Henry Cary Shuttleworth, a memoir;

George William Erskine Russell

HENRY CARY SHUTTLEWORTH

Faithfully yours
R Shuttleworth:

HENRY CARY SHUTTLEWORTH

𝔄 𝔐emoir

EDITED BY

GEORGE W. E. RUSSELL

LONDON
CHAPMAN AND HALL, Ld.
1903

" Clear brain and sympathetic heart,
  A spirit on flame with love for man,
Hands swift to labour, slow to part,
  If any good, since time began,
The soul can fashion, such souls can."

To the Reverend

MONTAGUE HENRY NOEL

In Affectionate Remembrance

of

St. Barnabas, Oxford

ITS WORK, ITS WORSHIP, AND ITS CLERGY

PREFATORY NOTE

THIS book is the work of several hands; and I have done little more than collect and arrange the material supplied by the kindness of others. Each period of Mr. Shuttleworth's life, and each department of his work, has been described by some friend who had special opportunities of close observation. As to the leading qualities of his moral and intellectual nature, it is interesting to note the concurrence of testimony from so many witnesses writing in complete independence of each other. The result of this combined handiwork does not profess to be more than a sketch; but even a sketch, if it has caught the characteristic features of its subject, may claim pardon for its roughnesses and imperfections.

The special thanks of those who read this Memoir are due to the Rev. Dr. Wace,

Rector of St. Michael's, Cornhill ; the Rev.
E. S. Shuttleworth, Rector of St. Stephen-
in-Brannell ; the Rev. C. N. Kelly, Rector
of St. Nicholas Cole Abbey ; the Rev. F. L.
Donaldson, Vicar of St. Mark's, Leicester ;
the Rev. W. E. Moll, Vicar of St. Philip's,
Newcastle-on-Tyne ; the Rev. G. W. Allen,
Vicar of Thornton-Steward ; the Rev. William
Russell, Vicar of Sunbury-on-Thames ; the
Rev. Thomas Hancock, of Harrow ; the Rev.
A. W. Hutton, of Richmond ; Dr. H. S.
Lunn ; Mr. Robert Snow ; and Mr. G. H.
Birch.

G. W. E. R.

All Souls' Day, 1902.

HENRY CARY SHUTTLEWORTH

THE Shuttleworths belong to the north of England. Robinson Shuttleworth was High Sheriff of Lancashire in 1795. His son, Thomas Starkie Shuttleworth, a freeholder of Preston, died in 1819, leaving a numerous family, of whom the fifth was Edward Shuttleworth (1806–1883). This Edward Shuttleworth took Holy Orders, and became in 1849 Vicar of Egloshayle—a pretty village near Wadebridge in Cornwall—where he spent the remainder of his life. He was a Tractarian in theology, a close ally of Bishop Phillpotts of Exeter, a noted preacher, and an enthusiastic musician. He married in 1849 Letitia Cary. Their elder son—christened Henry Cary—was born at Egloshayle on the 20th October, 1850, and throughout his life gloried in the fact that he was by birth a Cornishman.

Those who remember Henry Shuttleworth

B

in early youth describe him as a lively, intelligent and active child; strong in likes and dislikes; very keen about books, music and cricket; quick-tempered, warm-hearted, and not very easy to manage. When he was not quite nine years old, he was sent to Forest School, Walthamstow. He wrote in later life: "It so happened that I had inherited the family taste for music, and already, though so young, gave promise of a boy's voice of unusual range and quality. It was this that, after all, determined the school to which I was sent. . . . At Forest School in Essex there were some very desirable Choral Exhibitions. If I were fortunate enough to get one of these, it would reduce my school-fees by some forty or fifty pounds a year. To make a long story short, I got the Exhibition, which I held during my whole school-course."

Henry Shuttleworth was not happy at school. His own published Recollections, together with what he used to tell his friends at Oxford, seem to put this point beyond doubt. Yet he is remembered by schoolfellows as having been, at any rate towards the end of his time, "on the whole popular"; as having had "many friends"; as "loving the classics," acting excellently in the school-plays, and as having already begun to contribute verses to magazines.

But his chief glory then, as always, was his music. His younger brother, who was with him at Forest School, writes—

"He had a bass voice on its way, while, curiously enough, his treble voice was still capable of use for a time. We were singing Bishop's Glee, 'The Chough and Crow,' at one of our School-Concerts, when suddenly the treble soloist was taken ill, and could not sing. Henry was to sing the bass solo. So he did: but he sang the treble one also, to the great astonishment of the audience. This is no invention. I heard it."

Some of those who noted this remarkable aptitude in so young a boy, recommended him to devote himself to a musical career; but his father decided otherwise; and, though himself a Cambridge man, he consented that his son should compete for a "Dyke Scholarship," open to natives of the three western counties, at St. Mary Hall, Oxford.

Henry Shuttleworth spent more than eight years at Forest School. One of his juniors writes: "I remember his kind manner to me as a fresh boy, and his splendid voice in the chapel choir." In January 1869 he won the

Dyke Scholarship, and immediately went into residence at St. Mary Hall.

Two characteristic letters may here be inserted. On the 21st January, 1869, the Rev. Edward Shuttleworth writes thus to his successful son—

" My dearest boy,
        "Your mother has forwarded to me your telegram announcing your success. Thank God for it. Thank God who has given me a son who has commenced his career so honourably. I had given up all hope; for I did not think your work sufficiently *neat* to ensure success; specially when you were fighting with such formidable odds. May this be the presage of future success. May it spur you on to fresh exertions, and specially may you be humble-minded, and remember that all success is of God. . . .
                    " Your ever affect:
                        " E. SHUTTLEWORTH."

Eight years later Henry Shuttleworth wrote to a friend—

" I am so glad you like my dear old father. But I don't know who could help liking him, with his bright, cheery ways, his quaint old-world manners, and his simple earnestness. He is the truest and best Christian I ever knew; I only hope I may some day be half as good as

he is. I never see him or get a letter from him
without being touched almost to tears, by some
fresh proof of the simplest goodness and the
most self-denying humility. I have much to
thank God for, but most, I think, for having
been trained by such a father."

With regard to St. Mary Hall, Shuttleworth's brother, who was also a member of it,
writes—

" I have often thought it a great pity that he
did not go to a better college, and certainly he
should have taken the Honour School in
Moderations. But at St. Mary Hall men did
not go in for Honours; or, if they did, got no
assistance."

What Henry Shuttleworth was as an undergraduate we can gather from the testimony of
his contemporaries. One of them writes : " He
was my junior, and I remember him as a
specially bright and pleasant young fellow,
full of life and spirits, yet always having an
influence for good." Another describes him as
" shining, cheery, bright, young, enthusiastic,
and not very shy ; rather demonstrative, and
very full of words." Another says : " In those
years he was full of life and spirits, very intelligent, and very eager in whatever he undertook,
and a most devoted Churchman of the ritualistic

school. He did a good deal of Church work at
St. Barnabas. He was the life and soul of every
society he moved in. In fact, this characteristic
of overflowing life and spirits, and a certain
cocksureness, are my main recollections of him.
He was a perfectly pure-minded, good man,
and entirely sincere."

Yet another says : "He was the same
strenuous and energetic person as in after
years ; and, soon after coming up, commenced
early rising, telling his friends that he was trying to see how little sleep he could manage
with. The great feature in his undergraduate
life was his entire absorption in the ·Church,
Vicar, and work of St. Barnabas. His first
visit to that church filled him with enthusiasm ;
and he used to come back full of 'a splendid
sermon from the Vicar.'"

A clergyman of high standing in the north
of England, who was with Shuttleworth at St.
Mary Hall, says : "I remember remarking
either *to* him, or *of* him, in the days when he
seemed to be always engaged at St. Barnabas,
that I thought a man's duty to his friends should
lead him rather to books than to ritual, during
his short residence at Oxford." But this sage
counsel fell on rather unheeding ears. The
grand passion of working for the Church had

seized Shuttleworth for its own ; and he had neither leisure nor inclination for laborious reading. His natural sharpness and ready writing helped him in examinations, and in the Summer Term of 1873 he obtained a Second Class in the School of Theology.

The references to St. Barnabas Church in the foregoing extracts recall an event which had permanent effects on Shuttleworth's career, and which has not been without its influence on the general life of the Church of England.

St. Barnabas Church was built by the munificence of Mr. Coombe, of the University Press, in what was then considered one of the slums of Oxford, and was consecrated by Bishop Wilberforce on the 19th of October, 1869. "The opening of St. Barnabas," says one who remembers it, "may be regarded as epoch-making in the history of the Anglo-Catholic movement. The fine character and dignified bearing of the founder ; the preparatory work done by Mr. Hackman, the Vicar of St. Paul's, Oxford, from whose parish the district assigned to St. Barnabas was taken ; and the novel character of the Italian Basilica style of architecture—all seemed to open the way for a 'new departure'; and, when to these were added the strong personality of Mr. Noel, the first Vicar, and the marked though diverse gifts of his two curates, Rev. C. H. Moore and Rev. M. G. Davidson (all the three were Christ Church men), it was clear that something was bound to come of the new foundation. And so it turned out. The music indeed was severe in its simplicity, mostly Gregorian, all in unison, boys and men singing alternately. The ritual was, however, more ornate than anything before seen in Oxford, eucharistic vestments, silk and coloured, being used, as well as lighted candles, and even incense. The services were carefully rehearsed and went with a swing and precision that fairly astonished people; the sermons were in familiar language, pointed and short; and the Children's Service on Sunday afternoons was a novelty which attracted crowds. The roads leading down from Walton Street were alive with undergraduates, and other Oxford visitors, before and after each service. What arrested attention in those early years has become so common now that it has ceased to be interesting, and it may be difficult for a later generation to understand how it ever could have been interesting. But so it was; and with the attractive services was united a thorough working of the parish which Mr.

Noel had learned from Mr. Butler at Wantage, and the tone of all those who were associated in the work was one of cheery confidence, our idea being that we were rapidly transforming the dull old Church of England into her rightful ideal."

The church and the services thus described appealed powerfully to Henry Shuttleworth's rich and vivid nature. His musical gifts, his popular sympathies, and his theological traditions alike responded to the appeal. In the first year of his undergraduate life he associated himself with St. Barnabas and its work, and every year the union became closer. The Rev. M. H. Noel, the first Vicar of St. Barnabas, writes—

"My first acquaintance with him began by his offering to help us in the choir. Like David as a youth, 'he was ruddy, and withal of a beautiful countenance, and goodly to look to.' Moreover he was at home in manly exercises as in music. He soon proved himself to be very useful, and while still a layman he helped in the Sunday School, which was started before we had a Day School, and he was always ready to help the men and boys in any way he could in his spare time, being always thoroughly to be relied on for anything he undertook, and for the good tone he set. Seeing what an excellent Curate he would make, I secured him while still a layman, and he lived with myself and the other clergy in the Clergy House. He was ready to help in every possible way, taking classes of various kinds, in which he was most successful, as also in getting up entertainments, and in starting the *Parish Magazine*. In fact, it was in a large measure owing to his work as layman, deacon, and priest, that St. Barnabas became what it did in early days, and his love for St. Barnabas remained with him to the end."

In 1872 Shuttleworth went to live in St. Barnabas Clergy-House, and it was in the October of that year that the present writer, then a Freshman, first made his acquaintance. There sprang up between the two men an intimacy which lasted unbrokenly till they both left Oxford. What was Henry Shuttleworth like in those distant days ? School-boy slang rises naturally to the lips when one attempts to describe an undergraduate who was still at heart a school-boy. He was what boys call a bit of a " know-all ": there was nothing in the world that did not interest him, nothing about which he had not at least some information, nothing on which he had not a formed opinion. He

had what may be called the journalistic mind—
the knack of seizing the salient points, and of
saying, whether by instinct or by acquisition,
the exactly right thing about each topic as it
arose. As a matter of fact, he was already a
practising journalist, and habitually contributed
to one of the local papers. He was not a
specially good scholar, and not at all a profound
student; but he had the happy knack of reading so as to assimilate and apply what he read;
and no one excelled him in the art of beating
out his gold very thin. Music was of course
his special gift: there he was thoroughly at
home; there he was an admitted authority, at
once performer and critic He had little
taste for pure theology. He only went in for
the Theological School because his intensely
practical nature preferred to read what he
could turn to definite account the moment he
had taken his degree. Even then, though he
was a red-hot Ritualist, the authors to whom
he most inclined were not Newman or Faber,
but Ruskin and Kingsley. There was a
vigorous strain of Liberalism in his nature,
which rebelled against trammels and was im-
patient of grooves. In politics he was, as
later, a Christian Socialist, or Social Democrat
on Catholic lines. Like Arthur Stanton, he

"knew. no Radicalism except what he had sucked in from the breasts of the Gospel." His Liberalism, like Theodore Talbot's, was "a genuine love of the poor and helpless, founded on personal devotion to the Divine Workman of Nazareth." All his opinions—political, religious, social—were beliefs. He was absolutely confident in his own judgment. He called no man Master; and I cannot recall that, in those young and immature days, I ever heard him express a doubt. At that time there was a good deal of "Roman Fever" in Oxford. Most of us took it more or less severely. Some succumbed; many barely recovered, some had it very slightly. Shuttleworth seemed absolutely proof against the infection. Nothing Roman had the slightest attraction for him. He felt safe, happy, and confident where he was; and then, as always, he was profoundly convinced that the Church of England is the Society which is commissioned by God to proclaim His message to the English people.

As a companion he excelled. He was enthusiastic, buoyant, light-hearted, sanguine. His health was perfect, his activity untiring; his spirits were always at the highest pitch. Pain and weakness and fear and failure were to him unknown and unthinkable. Half-an-hour in his company was a certain cure for low spirits or morbid fancies. He was religious without being superstitious ; and lived from hour to hour in the unclouded sunshine of our Father's realized favour. After he went to live at St. Barnabas, he mixed very little in the general life of the University. He gave himself, body and soul, to the Church and parish ; his very devotion surrounding them with a halo of romance which the aspect of the locality would scarcely suggest. The undergraduate of whom at that time he saw most was the editor of this book ; who can never forget the long rambles over Hincksey and by the Upper River ; the eager discussions of everything in heaven and earth ; the generous schemes for setting the Universe right, the far-reaching plans of life, the keen delight in present enjoyment. Shuttleworth used to flare up into contagious enthusiasm over a fine bit of literature. He revelled in the physical beauties of Oxford and its setting. He was keenly alive to the historical and religious associations of the place. His sense of the ludicrous knew no bounds except those of kindness and charity.

But the basis of his whole nature, the root of all his activity, was his Arthur-like devotion to our Divine Master. Be it remembered that at this time he was still a layman; but he had worn the Lord's ephod from his earliest boyhood He was born, as we have already seen, in a Tractarian vicarage; and, after graduating as chorister and altar-server, he had passed on into the active and zealous performance of whatever ministries are possible to a layman. His ambition was to be a perfect Parish Priest; and he spared no pains in equipping himself for the work His speciality, already strongly marked, was his gift for dealing with boys and young men. To them he had a genuine devotion; on them he expended all the riches of his nature. He played their games; he invited them to his rooms; he lent them books; he corresponded with them in absence; he lived with them on terms of the frankest equality; and yet, all the time, he contrived to steer clear of spoiling them or making them forward and conceited, or losing his natural dignity, or lowering his social standard to theirs. And, indeed, it was not easy for boys or any one else to take a liberty with Shuttleworth. The "natural man" in him had a hot temper, and it blazed out into a sudden flame at the touch of impertinence or incivility.

The boys were his parish. His influence on

them was wholly good.   His manly and cheerful piety was the sworn foe of sickliness and effeminacy.   There are some who still remember the infinite pains and tact with which he drew back a lapsed lad to Confession and Communion ; the pleading letter in which he urged one who had been unjustly treated to kneel down before the crucifix, and consider his grievance in the light of the Passion ; his urgency in imploring an undergraduate friend to destroy, instead of posting, an ill-tempered letter.

To a nature so trained, and a life so ordered, entrance on to Holy Ministry made little outward change.   He was ordained Deacon in Advent 1873, and Priest a year later.   His social, educational, and parochial work went on just as before, though of course some fresh cares were added.   His preaching, vigorous, unconventional, passionately earnest, exuberantly rhetorical, was very popular.   " His name," says a contemporary, " had already become known in Oxford by the time of his ordination, and his first sermon at St. Barnabas was looked forward to as an event."

A well-known clergyman in the north of England writes—

" I went to Oxford in the October Term, 1875,

and became at once a member of the congregation of St. Barnabas, Oxford, and continued to
attend that church during all my life as an
undergraduate.   I shall always retain the most
sincere gratitude for all I learned at St. Barnabas.
The reverence and beauty of the services, and
the common-sense that pervaded all that was
said and done there, provided me with lessons
which I have found of the utmost value during
a ministry of twenty-three years to working
classes.   But I am not ashamed to say, in spite
of all the sneering that one hears now-a-days
about going to church for the sermon, that what
first of all attracted me to St. Barnabas was
the preaching of H. C. Shuttleworth, who was
acting as curate there when I first went up as
an undergraduate.   I had been brought up a
pronounced High Churchman, and, I hope, still
hold all the great truths which that school has
been the means of bringing back to the mind of
the Church.   But, even when I was only nine-
teen, I was beginning to feel dissatisfied with
my position, and to see that, true as was the
position of High Churchmen as to the import-
ance of the Church and Sacraments and a
dignified Worship, something more was needed
if these were to be brought home to the
consciences of the people.   I could not better

sum up my feelings with regard to Tractarianism than in the words of the prophet : 'The
bed is shorter than that a man can stretch
himself on it : and the covering narrower than
that he can wrap himself in it.' When I first
heard H. C. Shuttleworth preach, I felt at once
that here was a man who had felt what I was
feeling about Tractarianism, and who had got
some way out of the wood in which I then found
myself perplexed. I was at St. Barnabas
regularly during the year he preached there
before he went to St. Paul's, and I was never
disappointed. I always got something from
him which helped me along the road, and on
the occasions when I sought his help in Confession it was the same. I do not think he had
read F. D. Maurice then, and of course it would
not be true to say that he preached then as he
did afterwards in London, when we were both
committed to the Christian Socialist movement.
I rather think that Robertson of Brighton and
Stopford Brooke were the men who were
inspiring and helping him when he was preaching at St. Barnabas, but however that may
have been, he inspired and helped me. Some
of the sermons he preached then I shall never
forget, and I only wish he had left sufficient
material behind for them to be published. I

c

recall one for Whitsunday from Rev. xxii. 1, another for Ash Wednesday on Esau, 'He found no place for repentance,' another at the Dedication Festival on 'Be thou faithful unto death,' and one for Ascension Day, the text of which I have forgotten. If I may put in a word what Shuttleworth's preaching at St. Barnabas did for me, it was this : He made the dry bones of Tractarianism, as they had become for me at that time, live. He put me on the right track when I was in difficulties, and whatever service I may have been able to render in my ministry is due to a very large extent to what I learned from him in the sermons he preached at St. Barnabas, Oxford."

One of those who served with Shuttleworth at St. Barnabas adds this testimony to his parochial work—

" He provided a necessary element which the rest of us, so far as I remember, lacked. He was excellent with boys and young fellows, and could take part in their games. High Church clergymen of an earlier school would have felt that the putting on of flannels was derogatory to their priestly character : Shuttleworth had no such scruples. In the cricket-field he was as any other cricketer ; and although of course the parson who takes part in out-door games was

well known long before 1873, I think Shuttleworth was the first to combine chasubles before
the altar with flannels before the stumps. He
was also, I think, so far as High Churchmen
are concerned, the pioneer in that movement
for the establishment of boys and young men's
institutes and clubs wherein the association of
the members, whether lay or clerical, is of that
frank, free-and-easy, hail-fellow-well-met style,
now so common and so well understood. It is
a kind of work in which I have never been able
to take any useful part myself, and so I admire
it, in so far as I do admire it, from a respectful
distance. Certainly it has been an effective
instrument in the Church work of the last
quarter of a century ; and in its institution it
was largely due to Shuttleworth's magnetic
personality, pleasant, kindly humour, and to
the transparent goodness which inspired his
zeal."

In 1874 Shuttleworth's musical abilities pro-
cured him a Chaplaincy at "the Cathedral
Church of Christ in Oxford." He retained his
Curacy at St. Barnabas, and henceforth divided
his time between the Clergy-House and the
Chaplains' quarters in Christ Church. The
Rev. F. S. Donaldson, Vicar of St. Mark's,
Leicester, and formerly a chorister of Christ

Church, contributes these interesting recollections—

" His chaplaincy brought him into immediate
contact with the boy-choristers of the Cathedral,
and he immediately showed his lively interest
in them.   It was as one of these choristers that
I first knew him, and my impressions of him at
that period are recorded here faithfully just as I
remember them.   They are therefore those of a
boy of twelve in regard to one who was a sort
of dignitary set over us.

"We soon found out that Shuttleworth, though
a dignitary, *cared* for us.   The chaplains were,
upon the whole, respected rather than loved by
the choristers.   They were superior beings to
whom we took off our caps.   But they lived
apart, remote, inaccessible.

" Henry Shuttleworth changed all that.   He
brought into our life a breeze of vigorous joy
and friendship.   He was 'hail-fellow-well-met'
with the choristers immediately—and yet (as
will be seen later on) only within certain limits.
It was impossible for him then, as in later life,
to maintain the merely official relationship.   He
loved, and did not scruple to manifest it.

" The choristers were under the control of
the Chaplain Head-Master.   With that control
Shuttleworth never interfered.   But he could

not daily meet us at Cathedral, and in the rest of life ignore us. His ardent, loving temperament instantly brushed aside the official barriers which convention had placed between the choristers and the somewhat academic priests whom we knew mainly as officials at the services in Cathedral. From the very first, therefore, he became our friend.

"Truth to tell, the first impression he ever gave me was a very extraordinary one.

"He abruptly greeted us—a group of choristers playing in the Cathedral Quad—and returned our salutation by making at us a grotesque facial contortion! Imagine our amazement. No wonder we were puzzled about the new chaplain! And our wonder deepened when we discovered him to be a facial genius of the first rank, one whom even our colleague C——, the chorister-son of a famous comedian, could not surpass. Our wonder passed into admiration of the priest who enthralled us by his genius of face-making. It was to us a new and delicious experience—to have amongst us a chaplain who could beat C—— at his own trade!

"The new chaplain having thus broken the ice, rapidly secured our affections by still more acceptable tokens of friendship. Whatever good things Henry Shuttleworth ever had he invariably shared with others. We discovered his passion for sweets by his habit of soothing chorister-throats with them. A touch of nature makes the whole world kin. Here (sweets) was another touch of nature in the new chaplain, which endeared him to us. He liked sweets! and was fonder still of sharing them with us.

" But I need not say that these things were but symbols of real humanity and friendship. We soon discovered with whom we had to do —a priest, a gentleman, an elder brother, in whom there was no guile. The choristers were soon seekers after him for other things than fun and sweets and tea in his rooms. Friendship, sympathy, counsel and admonition soon became inextricably mixed up with the fun and frolic—the spiritual with the natural. It was in fact this admixture which made him as great a power with lads and youths as afterwards he became with men. We found him intensely human yet supremely spiritual.

" Here is a letter of this time which exhibits this paramount trait in his character. It is written to one of the choristers after he had left the Cathedral school for a great manufacturing town.

"'11 *Dec.* 1875.

"'Christ Church goes on much as usual, Term ends to-day, and men are going down in troops. I shall soon be going down myself, but no further than St. Barnabas, where, of course, I spend my Christmas. The boys are all well as far as I know. Johnny W—— is getting awfully fat. And as for you, I expect you are a walking barrel. A happy Xmas to you, and, dilectissime, don't let it be a Christmas without Christ for you—nothing but a time for parties and mistletoe and hot punch—though they are well enough in their way. On Christmas Day you shall read over a very favourite hymn of mine, 'Once in David's Royal City'—and as you read it think of

"'Your ever affectionate
"'PADRE.'

"His rooms at Christ Church and at the Clergy-House became our rendezvous in days when, unlike these, the choristers were left largely to their own devices. No Choir-House existed in those days. He never ceased to urge upon the Dean and Chapter the need of establishing a Choir-House for their choristers. Largely through his representations this reform was (about 1876) carried out, and a Choir-House was established and flourishes to this day. But in 1874 boys who came from places other than Oxford itself were placed in lodgings, well recommended no doubt, but without the discipline and supervision of the present Choir-House.

"Shuttleworth saw this and realized the danger, and, pending reform, met it in his own downright, frank, and thorough way. He *could* not be merely chaplain and sing the services. He gave us his friendship and devotion.

"He rarely crossed our path in college or out of it without a rush being made for him, and he pursued his way with a circle of boys hanging on to his hands or coat. To boys he became as a boy.

"Here is a letter, dated 1874, which one of those choristers has kept for eight-and-twenty years—

"'My dear but evil D——,
        "'You are a scaramouch, you are a gay deceiver. You are an entirely pestilent and abominable swab. . . .
"'In other words, why didn't you come this afternoon? I was careful to be disengaged ; I had laid in a stock of lollies and chocolate creams, and I sat patiently waiting for you, till at last I abused you frantically, parodied the first few verses of "Will he come?" and then went to sleep in my chair. The time went much more pleasantly while I was wrapped in the arms of Morpheus than if I had been

grinding with you—you small elf. Write and
explain yourself.'

"In dealing with the boys he was sternness
itself to all follies and faults, especially faults of
irreverence or guile. In 1875 he was acting
as superintendent of an examination for the
Diocesan prizes. He wrote to me and said,
'76 boys to look after and keep quiet. I saw
one looking very uncomfortable, so I guessed
he was cribbing, and went right at him. "What
have you got there?" in my sternest voice.
"N—n—nothing, sir," he said, holding his hands
up. "What are you *sitting* on?" I asked.
"Nothing, sir," was the answer. "Get up, and
let me see!" said I. He got up, and there was
a book out of which he had calmly been copying
his answers. I tore up his papers and turned
him out. Not a St. Barnabas boy, I am
thankful to say.'

"On another occasion I was rowing him
along on the Cherwell in a light boat. I caught
a crab and ejaculated, in school-boy fashion,
'D—n it.' I shall never forget the stern gaze
he fixed upon me, although he had only just
finished making a face at me!

"'My dear lad,' he said, after a few moments'
pause, '*never* defile your lips: they are

defiled by what you say, not by what you eat.'

"A reproof I have never forgotten.

"He was 'down on' all subterfuge, lying and boys' sins in a way that made us tremble with terror. In those young years we felt his power; afterwards only did we fully understand it. The secret lay in his deep humanity, controlled by and imbued with the loftiest principle. He first touched our hearts, and then ruled our wills for good. He heard in those days (*informally*, and doubtless formally as well, but that did not come within the writer's cognizance) many a boyish confession of sin and shame, and so saved many a soul alive.

"His power with boys and youths interests me profoundly as I look back upon it. He had his special friends of course, but never as 'favourites,' to the exclusion of the rank and file. He was as popular with the printers' boys at St. Barnabas as with the choristers of the Cathedral. He loved the lads and they loved him, yet there was never any slightest approach to sentimentality. The very word expresses all that he was *not* with boys. His friendship was a genuine human interest in them and their lives, their joys and sorrows, their play and work, their failures and their hopes. His

interest in the young led to the publication of
St. Barnabas Stories, which he wrote for Messrs.
Mowbray. They had a large sale, I believe,
and entranced me, and, I dare say, hundreds
of other boys.

"Scarcely a Sunday passed at St. Barnabas
without some of the choristers being present
to hear him preach. I was often one of a group
which wended its way to St. Barnabas.

"In 1875 he writes to an absent chorister—

"'*Christ Church, Nov.* 5.

. . . "'As for St. Barnabas, it goes on much
as usual. The number of Christ Church boys
who come down there now is quite surprising.
. . . I wish you had stayed here long enough
for me to teach you more on the subject
which we talked about so often. Don't forget
what I said. Some day perhaps it will bear
fruit. Say your prayers and try to live like
Jesus Christ : that, at least, is a point where all
agree.

"'God bless you, my dear boy. Don't let
Manchester life lead you wrong.'

"And in 1876—

"'*St. Barnabas, Oxford, Feb.* 23.

"'Christ Church has seen less of me, I think,
than it used to do, which is saying a good deal.
However, I often see some of the boys. A

regular regiment of them come to church here on Sunday afternoons and evenings. Walter and Buzz of course, and besides them H—— and H—— and H——, S——, G——, H—— and A—— are very constant. B—— hopes to be confirmed here in March, and is coming to me for preparation twice a week.'

"I will end this part of my narrative by a quotation from one of the Memorial Sermons preached at the time of his funeral—

"'Think of him as the young enthusiastic priest of seven-and-twenty years ago, whom schoolboys loved to honour and to hear, as he preached the everlasting Gospel. Think of him in his curacy at St. Barnabas at Oxford with rows of choristers before him, who, from twelve years old and upwards, left the Cathedral precincts and habitually walked a mile after one service, to sit at his feet and listen to his words at another. There are great preachers in our Church who would like to know that they could draw within their auditory, by natural attraction, ordinary schoolboys.'

"This was the heyday of Shuttleworth's ritualistic zeal, but he always wore his ritualism 'with a difference.' If he loved the Fathers, he loved Shakespeare too, if he read the Bible and said his Daily Office, he did not neglect his

Tennyson or Browning. His churchmanship
was strongly, deeply marked in these years,
but it never blinded him to the personal claims
of Christ. How wise are these words written
to a youth of sixteen who was just experiencing
the first strain of attractions other than those
of Church—

" ' I am sorry, of course, to hear you have not
kept up going to church. Chapel is not Church
and cannot be. But the first and chief thing
is to try and live like the Saviour when He
dwelt upon this earth; true and humble and
pure. It is important to be within His Church,
but it is more important to live as He did. If
you are not yet the first, you can try to be the
second. Write to me again.' "

In 1876 Shuttleworth brought his ministry
at Oxford to a close. In that year, at the suggestion of Dr. Liddon, he competed for a
Minor Canonry at St. Paul's Cathedral, and,
having been successful, immediately entered
on his new duties.

His departure from Oxford was deeply and
widely mourned. His farewell sermon at St.
Barnabas was preached amid deep emotion and
long remembered. On the 12th November,
1876, he wrote to a friend—

" The people were very kind and loaded me with presents. Not least the Christ Church boys gave me a really handsome pair of bronze candlesticks. If you had been among the troop that came down to my dismantled room in the Clergy-House and gave me the things! I could hardly say a word for fear of crying outright."

He keenly felt the pang of separation from Oxford : and, for some time after his arrival at St. Paul's, that pang was not healed. In November 1876 he wrote—

" Even now I can hardly realize that Oxford is my home no longer and that my place there is filled by others. It was the bitterest thing I have ever gone through to part from it all. . . . I came here on Friday week and found the rooms I am to occupy until my house is built, very cosy, and just like old college rooms, with panelled walls and immense fire-places. But they are small and very dark, as one might expect in London. My Oxford pictures are on the walls, and my books in their places, so it looks somewhat homelike, though at present I cannot help looking at it as Babylon and Oxford as Sion!"

He sorely missed the rural surroundings of beautiful Oxford.

" Chapter House, 12 April '77

" I don't much like being in London during spring-time. I have always been within an easy walk of the country before, and it is hard lines to see nothing from one's windows but the smoked bricks which mine command ; and to get no trees and fields and fresh air is dreadfully bothersome to me. Country birds like me should not come to town! I did enjoy my visit to Oxford. I always feel that I am going home when I go there. No other place will ever be the same to me, I think."

The same regret, the same passion, for Oxford is reiterated.

"June 18, '77.

" Oxford is like home to me. I often wonder how I could ever have left it. I must say that, though my work here grows in interest and value, I cannot yet feel for it what I felt for St. Barnabas or Christ Church. As one of my young men here told me, my heart is buried at Oxford."

The removal from Oxford to St. Paul's marked an important stage in the history of Shuttleworth's life. One of his colleagues at the Cathedral contributes these interesting recollections—

" It was, I think, in the early days of the autumn of 1876 that I first met Henry Cary

Shuttleworth. We had been elected to Minor
Canonries at St. Paul's (the first under the
newly-constituted statutes) in the previous July.
We came up by mutual arrangement to lunch
together at Dr. Liddon's, and to have the
opportunity of talking over with him the possibilities of the new work which it was hoped
would open out in connexion with the Cathedral. He was not entirely a stranger to me,
even if we had not actually met before : for I
knew his younger brother at Forest School,
and I had frequently heard about him from
my own brother, who had known him in
Oxford. We were both rather enthusiastic at
the prospect before us, not merely, I think,
because it was in connexion with St. Paul's,
but because St. Paul's was then under the
guidance of R. W. Church (Dean), and H. P.
Liddon, J. B. Lightfoot, and Robert Gregory
(Canons) : and we both felt what a privilege
it was to be associated with such men. What
I remember, however, being particularly struck
with in Shuttleworth was his enthusiasm at the
prospect of working among the young men in
the great warehouses which surrounded St.
Paul's. 'That is my strong point,' he con-
fidently affirmed, and no one will venture to
say that he was mistaken in this. For he

certainly had a magic power of attracting young
men, as was shown soon after by the number
he collected around him and succeeded in
holding together till the end.

"As the new Residentiary Houses in Amen
Court were not yet built, we both of us at first
took up our temporary residence in the Chapter-
House, where also Dr. Lightfoot had rooms
when in residence at St. Paul's. Shuttleworth
had rooms on one side, and I on the other:
with a kitchen (and a kindly old housekeeper
to preside over it) in common. We had our
meals together in one another's rooms by
alternate weeks.

"As—apart from the services in the Cathedral, which were not then so numerous as they
were later — there was comparatively little
definite work to do at first (for the new work
could only be developed gradually), he felt the
contrast with his active life at St. Barnabas,
Oxford, very keenly. And I shall never forget his delight, when after a few weeks—the
occasion was a *Conversazione*, to which a
number of young men were invited to meet
some of the Cathedral clergy in the Chapter-
Room—definite arrangements were made for
classes and other work: and a real start seemed
likely to be effected. And indeed before long,

D

what with invitations to preach out, the Editor-
ship of *My Sunday Friend*, classes, and so
on, he was involved in a vortex of labour
which was sufficient to satisfy even his energy.
I used to think (perhaps wrongly) that his
talents lay on the surface rather than in great
depth : but his buoyancy of spirit, his self-
confidence, when needed, his readiness, his
great fluency made a deep impression upon
me : and indeed (by contrast with my own
lack of such gifts) used often to force upon me
a conviction of my own unfitness for the particular work in view. If, however, I spoke of
this to him, he used laughingly to say, that his
fluency was only due to some Irish or Celtic
blood that flowed in his veins, and went for
nothing.

"But although there were traits in his character (apart from his ability) in such marked
contrast with my own, we lived together under
the same roof for about three years on the most
affectionate terms. and even if there were
certain points on which we mutually agreed
to differ, I cannot remember that we ever
had anything like a quarrel, or even an unkind
word He was too kindly and generous-
hearted—and, for the matter of that, generous-
handed too—to give any occasion for this."

At the time when Shuttleworth joined the staff of St. Paul's, the Cathedral had already awoke from its long slumber; and, under the guidance of Church and Liddon, was beginning to claim its proper place as the principal seat of Christian worship in the Diocese of London. It was in 1878 that the Three Hours' Service was held for the first time in St. Paul's, Shuttleworth conducting it, and speaking to an enormous congregation. But it must be confessed that the authorities of the Cathedral, though entirely admirable on the religious and ecclesiastical sides, were a little lacking in human sympathies, and more than a little indifferent to the material and political claims of Labour, to the various enterprises of Social Reform, and to the soul of good which lurks even in the gross evils of Secularism. In this environment, a man of Shuttleworth's ardent temperament, just awaking to a sense of its peculiar powers, could scarcely be happy. He would not and could not be a mere Mass-Priest. The recitation of the Daily Office gave no adequate scope to his social fire. All round him he saw, with astonished eyes, the obvious and neglected opportunities for Social Service. Conventionalism and formality, starch and restraint, he had always despised; and his

sense of what was due to the dignity of the
great Church which he served (and no man
ever had that sense more strongly) did not
suggest that he ought to stand aloof from the
vigorous currents of economic, political, and
religious enquiry which were eddying round
the Dome. He therefore flung himself with
characteristic energy and self-forgetfulness into
a variety of enterprises which are described in
the following pages by one who shared and
stimulated his activities—

"In the year 1872 God showed how severe
a controversy He had with our English Church
and Commonwealth, as I then thought and
still think, by taking away from us Frederick
Denison Maurice in the fulness of his powers.
Though I had been many years in Holy Orders,
and had served populous parishes in and near
London, I had lived in a kind of isolation, for
I had nowhere come as yet in contact with any
brother-priest who felt in what a peculiar sense
Maurice had been sent forth by God to our
Church and Nation. I remember how I went
about after his death with the despondent
groan of the People of God in my heart : 'We
see not our signs, there is not one prophet
more : no, not one is there among us that
understandeth any more.' The best clergy

whom I knew were men of splendid zeal and
devotion, but they seemed to regard the
Church only as one denomination amongst
others, as like them having her end in herself, and her task in the cultivation of an
individual religiousness: as differenced from
the others mainly in being Catholic, and not
being Puritan, Methodist, or Rationalist, and
in possessing the unbroken Apostolic order and
common worship.   There appeared indeed to
be some visible tokens of a national repentance
in the new Common Schools which were becoming such conspicuous objects in the land-
scape of London.   But there was also the fear
that the sudden zeal of the English Commonwealth for the better schooling of all its children
had something in it of the service of Mammon
as well as of the service of the Father; for we
daily heard promises that the Capitalism of
England would be better furnished to compete
against the Capitalism of sister nations if we
had a caste of cheap wage-slaves as intelligent
and skilled as they had.   The aim of a national
schooling, even in the judgment of so humane
a Liberal as John Bright, was to enable a boy
or girl individually to 'get on,' or to obtain
individual wealth; which, in the Empire of
Mammon, is mostly effected by pushing their

neighbours 'off.' The aim of schooling, according to the almost invariable language of the charters of our old English Free Schools—which were composed under the inspiration of the Church—was to enable the scholar to grow up 'a good member of this Church and Commonwealth.' The founders of the old Free Schools looked at civil and ecclesiastical life from the standpoint of the Catechism. Boys and girls were sent to school to learn how to do their duty to their Common Father and to all their neighbours.

"The Catholic Church in every nation and parish, falls into apostasy when it acts as if it existed for itself. 'Of His own will begat the Father us, with the Word of truth, that *we* should be a kind of first-fruits of His Creatures.' Christ, His Son and Word, is the only Head of the Church because He only is the Head of Humanity. The Church must be on every man's side.

"No English priest in our time was more richly possessed by this doctrine of St. James than was Henry Cary Shuttleworth. He acted upon it himself. he taught it to others. He did not learn it directly from Maurice, as he once told me, but from Kingsley, whose genial temper seemed to live again in Shuttleworth.

'It is to Kingsley,' said he, as we were walking from his house in Amen Court to St. Paul's Cathedral, 'that I owe my deliverance.' Kingsley, as was inevitable, sent him to Maurice. Yet he never came into any personal contact with either of these ever-memorable teachers.

"Amongst others who were exercising more or less influence over his thinking and acting, when I first knew him, I may mention Dr. Church, the Dean of St. Paul's, whom he so deeply revered ; Ruskin, Browning, and William Morris ; the late John Oakley, afterward Dean of Manchester, that intrepid and sensible combatant for social righteousness ; and beyond all the rest, the Rev. Stewart Headlam.

"Before I knew Henry Shuttleworth personally, I read and heard of his appearance at the Church Congresses, where he acquired the beginnings of his later popularity. His ready and masculine language, his facile grip on whatever matter he took in hand, his sunny countenance, his kindly humour, always secured him an eager welcome. At the first, as at the last, the sight of him, and still more his speech, seemed to gladden and quicken his audience. If he was known to be at a meeting, calls of 'Shuttleworth ! Shuttleworth !' were sure to be raised when the discussion was thrown open. The year before he came to London, at a meeting of the Oxford branch of the English Church Union, the Rev. Malcolm MacColl, his friend from beginning to end, upon the invitation of the learned and saintly Canon Bright, addressed the members upon Sacerdotalism and Lawlessness. The eager young curate of St. Barnabas, who remained a member of the English Church Union until his death, leaped to his feet and read a printed notice announcing that Bishop Colenso would preach at Carfax on the next Sunday. Henry denounced the 'lawlessness' of the clergyman who had invited 'a deposed and excommunicated Bishop' to preach in the City Church of the Cathedral town, and he moved and carried a resolution to forward a protest to the Bishop of Oxford, begging him to prevent the scandal. No one would have been more amused than himself, two or three years later, at his own apparition as an implicit prosecutor. It interested me, because I had been asked if I would take a place of some honour and interest in the South African Church, which I refused, not only because I had much more care for the national heart of England than for its imperialist extremities, but also because I agreed with *both* the opposed parties in the South African Church—the Metropolitan and his Suffragan of Natal—and could not bring myself to serve one against the other, nor to regard Catholicity and the critical spirit as natural enemies.

"The next year, 1876, was that in which Henry Shuttleworth became one of the clergy of the Church of London. It was the year in which the still-national heart of England was astir and petitioning, and the wisest of English patriots, thinkers, scholars and historians were taking up arms against the turgid Bill of our semi-oriental Prime Minister, Mr. Disraeli, for manipulating our old English Kingdom into a brand-new Empire, after the model of Asiatic Imperialism. His ideal of a monarch was not an Alfred, but a Nebuchadnezzar, and his project was welcomed with delight by the Yellow International, which had its centre in the City of London. At the same time the mercy of God towards our English Church and Commonwealth had resuscitated the Christian Socialist spirit in the very place where Satan's seat was. These two contrary spiritual forces were contending in the air of London when Henry Shuttleworth was fetched from Oxford to his work as a Minor Canon in the Cathedral of London. It was not long before he made the great renunciation, proved that he believed the *Magnificat* sung in the modern Church of London every day, declined to join the hosts of the proud, the mighty, and the rich, and enlisted with his stainless sword in the service of the poor, the humble and the meek that had no helpers.

"My acquaintance with Henry Shuttleworth began at the monthly gatherings of the London Junior Clergy Society, and was soon increased and deepened by our community in work as members and lecturers of the Guild of St Matthew. I used also to meet him in the year 1881 on the executive council of 'The Curates' Alliance,' a society founded by the Rev. R. H. Hadden, who was at that time a hot young ecclesiastical reformer, and the first founder and editor of *The Church Reformer*, and is now a respectable West End clergyman. Henry Shuttleworth was always no less anxious than Headlam and I were to prevent the Curates' Alliance from being degraded into a mere trades-union of clergymen who had failed to get 'preferment.' We saw that the establishment of a certain number of individual clergymen, instead of the establishment of the whole estate of the clergy, was a greater injury to the congregation of Christ

than it was to this or that particular clergyman; because in our corrupt modern society
the patrons mostly represented the anti-social
interests of Mammon, Caste, or Party, and therefore were not likely to nominate to the Bishops
the very sort of priests whom the Church under
conditions of freedom would be certain to
choose for herself. I remember our contest
over a resolution in the hospitable vestry of St.
Botolph's, Bishopsgate, on behalf of the right
and duty of every Congregation of the Lord in
the appointment of its priests and deacons.
The Curates' Alliance, alas! like so many similar
societies which had preceded it, and others
which have followed it, came to an end because
it knew not how to touch the heart and conscience of the whole Church.   It is only possible
for the unbeneficed clergy to touch the conscience of their step-mother the Church, and
compel her to treat her labourer as worthy of
his hire, by showing that they are more concerned by the spiritual grievances of the elect
People of God than by the worldly grievances
of a Clerical profession.

" The Curates' Alliance was virtually one of
the many outcomes of the London Junior Clergy
Society. Another outcome of that Society, at
which I also frequently met Henry Shuttle-

worth, was the monthly supper of the Clerical
Social Club.   That Club was a benevolent
project of the Rev. G. W. Allen, that excellent
fisher of men, who hoped that it might serve as
a net for catching fresh young deacons and
presbyters of liberal tendencies and save them
from falling a prey to the poachers of the
religious world, the flesh, and the devil.   It
cannot be said to have prospered very widely
in its object : it caught few of the young clergy :
but it educated the older clergy who supped and
smoked together, for it brought them under the
preaching of democratic wage-workers, agnos-
tics, dissenters, spiritualists, and other sorts of
guests, wisely invited by G. W. Allen, mostly
of a kind not inclined to favour the English
parson."

A word should now be said about Shuttleworth's connexion with the London Junior
Clergy Society.

"The work of the London Junior Clergy
Society, founded in December 1873, deserves
some notice here, because it brought Henry
Shuttleworth into contact and discussion with
so many of his brother-clergy who were most
to influence his later career, and to become his
constant friends and helpers.   Moreover, the
London Junior Clergy Society was holding an

altogether unique place in the history of the
Church of London, and of the Londonized
parishes of the Churches of Rochester and
Winchester at the time when he became one of
the London clergy.

"The principal aim of this Society was to lay
hold of the young clergy after their ordination ;
to rescue the lonely from isolation, and to
inspire the gregarious to devote to the Common
Church the fresh zeal which they would otherwise be tempted to give up to party. It declared
no open war against either of the parties by
whose wranglings the Church was divided; and
in that sense the Society may perhaps be
regarded as a nursery for those whom Henry
Shuttleworth afterwards described as the
'Fourth Party' in the Church, which is neither
High nor Broad, but a compound of the two.
Its promoters saw that bondage to a party
tended to enfeeble and darken the common
catholic, national, and parochial witness of the
clergy. A young clergyman, fascinated and
fettered by one of the parties before and after
his ordination, came in time to prefer the interests of his party to the common good of the
Church, or else so blindly to confuse the two
things as to imagine that every victory of his
party must be a profit to the Church. God

had already constituted us unto one common
and united clergy by His own act in our ordination ; and there was something hopeful in the
organization of a free fellowship to bring
together for common counsel the fellow-clergy
of London, who were too inclined by individual
preference for one special aspect of truth, or by
too exclusive contemplation of what is ideal in
their own party and what is corrupt in other
parties, to keep as far as possible from one
another.

" Though the London Junior Clergy Society
was started mainly for the help of the newly-
ordained deacons and priests, its membership
was open to all the beneficed and licensed clergy
of the three dioceses, whether old or young.
Here not a few of us first found, as I did, a
comradeship and community of purpose which
brought a new gladness and freedom into our
lives as clergymen.   When I lost my licence, as
I did soon after I became a member, the Society
did not deprive me of its membership.   The
original founder and promoters of the London
Junior Clergy Society were Dr. Liddon ; Dr.
Lightfoot, afterwards Bishop of Durham ; Dr.
Barry, of King's College, afterwards Bishop of
Sydney ; A. W. Thorold, Bishop successively
of Rochester and Winchester ; G. H. Wilkin-

son, afterwards Bishop of Truro, and now of St. Andrews; Charles Kingsley, Henry Shuttleworth's 'master,' then Canon of Westminster; Llewellyn Davies, the honoured keeper of so large a portion of the treasures and traditions of Maurice; the energetic Erskine Clarke, instinct with organizing zeal, formerly of Derby, then Vicar of Battersea, who sent Shuttleworth to the Church Congress as correspondent of *Church Bells*; lastly, Dr. Vaughan, Master of the Temple, the amiable apostle of tameness. He was a valuable aid, because a considerable number of young clergymen passed under his training. They were characteristically known as 'Vaughan's Doves'; though a falcon was for a while included in the Vaughan pigeon-house, in the person of Stewart Headlam, who received from him the most astounding counsel that ever an old priest gave to a young one. Upon the removal of two of these Vice-Presidents, one vacancy was filled by the present Archbishop of York; the other by Dr. Littledale, a scholar whose popular pen had gained him in many respects a greater power, and certainly a wider influence upon the clerks and warehousemen, and the so-called 'Lower Middle Class,' than most of his colleagues could exercise. Of all these prelates and priests, only

four are still living—Archbishop Maclagan,
Bishops Barry and Wilkinson, and Rev. Llewellyn Davies. Mr. Wilkinson, as I believe, was
the moving spirit and central soul of the Society.
One of the duties of a Vice-President was to
address the members at a quarterly celebration
of the Holy Eucharist, after which it was our
custom to breakfast together. We were then
so many in number that I remember hearing a
workman exclaim, as he saw us flocking out of
some hotel or restaurant near St. Paul's Cathedral: 'Whatever are all these parsons up to?'
It has been said, but I know not how truly,
that the estimable Liberationist politician, Mr.
Carvell Williams, virtually disestablished us.
He unconsciously dealt the Society its death-
blow by his new Marriage Bill. Three o'clock
in the afternoon was our hour of meeting; but
when matrimony in the afternoon had become
legal and customary, many a curate was kept
away from our meetings because he had to stay
in his parish to officiate at marriages. Perhaps
the gradual thinning of the attendance was
rather a product of the negligence, or want of
interest, on the part of our Fathers-in-God,
who did not see the necessity of such meetings
of clergy upon a purely catholic ground, and
would not counsel their newly-ordained Deacons

and Priests, as their predecessors had done, to join the Society.

"Young Crawfurd Tait, the lovable son of the Archbishop, used to be frequent in his attendance, and some had a notion that he reported at Lambeth Palace the things he heard at St. Martin's Vestry-Hall. Archbishop Tait was a Scot, a business-like prelate, but not an enthusiastic one. We saw little in him of that impassioned love for the English Church which set on fire the fatherly heart, glorified the very face, and at last consumed the life of his successor, Archbishop Benson. The London Junior Clergy Society enjoyed in turn the hospitality of both Primates at Lambeth Palace. I can see Archbishop Benson now, as he laid his hand upon Henry Shuttleworth's shoulder after breakfast at Lambeth, and said: 'I love you for your father's sake,' and then added, with his ever-kindly smile, as if he suddenly remembered what the young priest was attempting for the Church of England, 'and for your own.'

"After various brave endeavours, on the part of a few, to keep the London Junior Clergy Society alive, it proved to be past recovery, died, and was reverently buried. I have heard that a society is extant which takes the same

E

name, and has a more numerous membership, but is not inspired with the like patriotic care for our own native English Church and Commonwealth. I am told that it concerns itself more about the prosperity of the extremities than about the healing of the sore heart and rotting body of England. Some at least of its members—I would not be so unjust as to say all—seemed to me to be drinking deeply out of the mercantile cup of Babylon, and to be tinctured with the anti-national and anti-Christian temperament of a so-called 'Christian Imperialism.'

"The London Junior Clergy Society was in its third or fourth year of age when Shuttleworth joined it, and when I first saw his happy face. I imagine that Dr. Liddon, whose influence had brought him from Oxford to St. Paul's Cathedral, advised him to become a member. The first paper which he read before the London Junior Church Society indicated the direction in which his face was set. 'Christian Socialism' was its title and subject. It did not exhibit much familiarity with original sources, and its details were trustfully borrowed from others: but it did exhibit his own heart of sympathy with all those that are desolate and oppressed, his resolution to dare and do everything he could as their spokesman; the precise knowledge of their wrongs and needs which he had acquired by his own personal study and research, his clear sight that English society was out of joint because it was not obeying Jesus Christ. I have a vivid recollection of this and other of his appearances amongst us. He burst into the old Vestry-Hall of St. Martin's-in-the-Fields like a bright ray of sunshine, cheery and radiant, fresh in countenance and in speech. So ruddy, alert, and vigorous was he in his young manhood that it was hard to think of him as living in the foggy airs of the City of London: he looked rather as if he had just come from the fields and woods, and had been long enjoying a sportsman's out-of-door life. The impression which he made upon me at the first he retained to the end: even when he was personally weighted with cares, he appeared to bring with him, wherever he appeared, a fund of joy and strength for others."

Another Society with which Shuttleworth was closely connected was the Church Reform Union.

"Shuttleworth did not join the Church Reform Union because he wanted a fellowship broader than that of the English Church, for

he knew that it was not possible for human art
to invent any fellowship in England equally
broad.   But he was by instinct a reformer ;
and it was always a joy to his generous heart
to engage in common discussion with serious
men of all sorts of opinions, guesses, and projects concerning the best ways of mending
whatever was confessedly out of joint in the
Church or the Commonwealth.   From Pusey
and Maurice he had learned exactly the same
lesson—namely, that sects can never be con-
verted into churches—neither by a prodigious
increase of their own adherents, nor by an
Act of Parliament disestablishing the Church
and substituting some sect, or fanciful amalgamation of sects, in her stead.   Yet though he
knew it to be as impossible to make a new
Catholic Church as to make a new sun or
moon, he had a Christian friendliness towards
all the sects, because he saw them to be historical products of the piety and sincerity of
Christian souls who had mostly been driven
to experimentalize upon the creation of some
new kind of a 'church' by the apostasy or
corruption which they saw, and many of
them suffered under, in that Church which
the Eternal Word of God had once for
all created.   He had two points of contact

with the programme of the Church Reform Union: (1) He shared in its perception that half the religious and ecclesiastical troubles in England are due to our continued establishment of the feudal Patron, and might be amended by restoring the original democratic establishment of the whole Church. (2) He was consequently ready to contend for its proposition that the Commonwealth should be urged to set itself upon the Liberation and Establishment of the Church. These kindred acts, each of which is incomplete without the other, could only be effected by transferring to the Church the free and full exercise of the spiritual rights and duties which inherently belong to her, but whose use and exercise are now withheld from her by the Patrons. But what did the Church Reform Union understand by the Church? I recollect how much consultation and correspondence he and I had with one another over this point. I had served for a time as the very inefficient secretary of the Church Reform Union, and had given it the rather unpalatable advice that it should put itself into communication with the English Church Union, as the only ecclesiastical society from whence it could possibly hope to enlist any young and enthusiastic regiment of lay soldiers. Its work would then have been to convince ardent and religious souls that the election of the parish priest by the Church (that is, by the organic local congregation, by the parish as a People of Christ) would involve no contradiction to the primitive faith and permanent constitution of the Catholic Church, but was a most logical inference from the one, a most unnatural development of the other.

" The Church Reform Union, however, was not so much a Church society as a Clericalist society. Some of its promoters were politicians, some were priests, some were dissenting ministers. Half of these promoters, perhaps most of them, seemed to be more eager about the private concerns of the minister than the common concerns of the Church. The question was, suppose the Patrons should be disendowed of their feudal autocracy over the parishes as the nominators of their clergy, and the parochial congregation be established in their stead as free electors of its own clergy—what sort of man should the parish be allowed to prefer as its rector or its assistant curates ? One of the projects of the Church Reform Union, perhaps its darling project, was that the 'clergyman' of its Church in the future need not hold the Catholic Faith, and need not be a Catholic

priest. Their notion of 'Reform' was pre-
dominantly clericalist, and consequently anti-
sacerdotalist : they wanted an Act for the relief
of a clerical class from the obligations of the
Act of Uniformity, rather than an Act for the
Relief of the whole organic People of Christ.
Such purely class and clericalist scheme had no
fascination for the broad and democratic mind
of Henry Shuttleworth. 'The Act of Uniformity,' wrote he, 'was originally a measure
of Relief, and was intended to secure to the
People certain rights which the Puritans denied
them.' In 1886 Mr. Albert Grey, M.P. (now
Lord Grey), at a notable conference in the
Charterhouse upon his scheme for 'Church
Boards,' ingenuously confessed that the first
step towards including all Englishmen within
the Church would have to be the driving of all
High Churchmen out of the Church. That
amazing politician fancied that the right trick for
raising the body of the Church (or whatever he
meant by the 'Church') from its imminent death,
was to stamp out all the promising signs of life
which were astir in it. Henry Shuttleworth
was too sane and practicable a man to have
much patience with this amateur and drawing-
room 'Reformation.' What patience he had,
he then and there lost. I can see him now, as

he started up indignantly and declared that he could not join in their movement for ship-wrecking the Church. 'Except these abide in the Ship,' said he, 'ye cannot be saved. If you deliberately cut yourselves off from that school of thought, you are signing your own death-warrant. You are making it impossible for High Churchmen to work with you, and by so doing you are ruining a work which at the outset promised so well.'

"Amongst the Dissenting friends of the Church Reform Union, two were then promi-nent, the venerated Dr. Martineau and the Rev. G. S. Reaney, whose Christian Socialist spirit led him afterwards out of the narrow bonds of Independence into the broad freedom of the Church. He once asked us to accept him as a member of the Guild of St. Matthew, which we should thankfully have done; but we could not admit him as a clergyman, which would have been disloyal to the Catholic Church: hence it could only then be done upon the ground that he was already constituted a lay-man of the Church by the fact of his baptism, and we shrunk from even seeming to cast any slur upon the validity and sincerity of his ministry. It is the business of the whole Church of God, and not of any private men or

separated societies, to say who are her clergy,
and how they are become Deacons, Priests, or
Bishops. He afterwards resigned his eminent
post and wide popularity as a Dissenting
minister, and became the curate of a Kentish
parish, and died prematurely a vicar at Green-
wich. Dr. Martineau, with all his clearness
of vision in the region of pure thinking, had so
meagre a perception of the fundamental points
of division between an Erastian and a Catholic
conception of the union of Church and State,
as to say, that if the State were to establish
and endow the Church Reform Union's programme, toleration within it would be extended
to such men as Henry Shuttleworth. 'Mr.
Shuttleworth,' said he, 'could retain all his
Ritualism.' It was an odd notion of the real
mind and standing of H. C. Shuttleworth. He
did not look upon ritual as a religious indulgence
for himself, though his poetical, artistic, and
historical sense might incline him to like it.
He had little sympathy with such ritualists as
would divide a parish by a clamour for the
enjoyment of their own individual 'privileges.'
He could have done his work without ritual as
well as with it, if he had found it to be really a
flag of Party, or a stumbling-block to the whole
People of God."

The Guild of St. Matthew was founded in 1877, with the twofold object of "justifying God to the people," and of dealing with all political and social problems in the spirit of the Divine Incarnation.

"It was as a foremost and ardent lecturer of the Guild that the natural popularity which Henry Shuttleworth had brought up from Oxford to London, and which he so easily increased here, alike amongst clergy and lay-folk, had first to pass through the fire. Many of his 'High Church' patrons and admirers were alarmed, for his own sake, no less than for the sake of the Party, when they saw this bright young priest, with such prospects of worldly gain in the Church of God, openly declare himself to be a Socialist. His qualification of the thing 'Socialism' with the adjective 'Christian' merely served to increase their horror and regret.

"For according to the prevalent notion of the High and Low Parties dividing the Church, it was not a counsel of God that His poor people should be led forth out of the English Egypt; while according to the opinion of the party which contended for broader freedom of thought in the drawing-rooms and studies of the well-to-do classes, it was tolerable for a clergyman to prove that Moses and Aaron never existed, but intolerable for him to discern in Moses and Aaron the first founders of trades-unions, social democratic agitators against the interests of Mammon, preachers of Home-Rule for Israel, and patriots who stirred up a nation to free itself from the Imperialist misrule of Pharaoh."

Shuttleworth joined the Guild of St. Matthew in 1880, four years after he had been brought up from Oxford to St. Paul's Cathedral. "At the Leicester Church Congress, in 1880, where he spoke in behalf of the Drama, he was introduced by the Chairman as a 'Minor Canon of St. Paul's,' but at the Newcastle Church Congress in 1881, as a 'Member of the Guild of St. Matthew.' He there and then told the assembled clergy and layfolk what kind of work the Guild was attempting to do amongst the Secularist workmen of London For in that hopeful generation, when the Devil had scarcely begun to infect the poor in our dear fatherland with his anti-Christian plague of Imperialism, there were wage-workers, serious enough to be Secularists, too serious to be gamblers and jingoes, and with sufficient love for their neighbours and their nation to look for some great Revolution like that promised by the Blessed Virgin to the poor, the humble,

and the hungry, and still professedly anticipated
by the Church in the daily recitation of her
Magnificat.   In that evangelical anticipation,
he as a believing Churchman, and good men
who never dreamed of going to church, had
a common godly ground for faith and work;
and it was the Guild of St. Matthew which
brought them often into fellowship and controversy.   It was in the year 1881 that he joined
with others in signing the Guild's appeal to the
Clergy on 'The Church and Secularism.'

"Certain it is that Henry Shuttleworth had
more to risk than the rest of us had.   He had
the best of characters to lose ; some among us
had a bad character in this present evil world :
others were too unknown to carry on them
either a good or a bad label.

" Henry Shuttleworth turned a deaf ear to all
counsels of prudence addressed to him by his
well-meaning patrons and friends.   I recollect
what efforts they made to 'save' him in the
end of the year 1883, shortly before his nomina-
tion to St. Nicholas Cole Abbey, when he
and his friends, through his influence, had
obtained the use of the sacred halls of the
English Church Union for a series of Lent
Conferences.   He was to open the course with
'The Church and Modern Society.'   When it

was found that all the lecturers were to be
'Christian Socialists,' High Churchmen and
Low Churchmen, the Catholic and the Evangelical, suddenly found out that they were not
such foes to each other as they had fancied.
They discovered that they had at least a
negative bond of union in their common horror
of that Socialism which neither of them understood.   *The Rock* exposed 'The fact that there
is an alliance utterly inexplicable, between the
Ritualists and the Revolutionists.'   A widely-
read 'Society' paper denounced Henry Shuttleworth for his offences against the world,
the flesh, and the devil, and entreated him to
repent and amend before it was too late.
'There was a time,' said the Society journalist,
'when Minor Canon Shuttleworth gave promise
of being an ornament to the Church of England.
Evil communications corrupt good manners.
Mr. Shuttleworth, we are afraid, is no longer a
coming man—unless he contemplates giving up
Christianity for the sake of cultivating Socialism.
The two cannot grow together.   But it may
be doubted whether, as a Socialist leader,
Mr. Shuttleworth would be a success.'   The
'Society' scribe, after he had done scolding,
turned to cajoling.   'Would it not be better to
draw back now,' asked he, 'before Mr. Shuttle-

worth has helped to encourage one of the worst movements and some of the most dangerous men in London? He has a reputation to lose. Is he prepared to lose it for the sake of joining in the cry for the abrogation of the Eighth Commandment?' 'If insurrection should break out in England,' screamed *The Rock*, 'it will be due, and largely indeed, to the clerical and other fire-brands, Mr. Shuttleworth and his friends, who are seeking to propagate what they call Christian Socialism.' The Hon. C. L. Wood (the present Lord Halifax) attempted to quiet the two angry worlds of Society and Religion by assuring them that the loan of the English Church Union rooms had been obtained through a misapprehension, without consulting the council or himself, and that permission to use them had been withdrawn.

" It may be conceived from the excerpts I have given that Shuttleworth's accession to the Guild of St. Matthew won for it an increase of power and reputation which it would take a long time to win without him. The gain of so popular a priest as an eager and a frequent lecturer did more for the Guild than the gain of hundreds of sleeping members, and an endowment by a millionaire, could have done.

" Money and multitude are such feeble forces, but one sincere good man is a force so powerful, in the Kingdom of Christ. I can remember how sedulously he lectured at Freethought Institutes, Liberal Clubs, and Secularist Societies from 1881 to 1883, often on Sunday nights after evening service, upon ' Parsons and the People,' ' Some reasons why I am not a Secularist,' ' Heaven and Hell,' ' The Priesthood and Popular Progress,' ' Fear God, Honour the King,' ' Christianity and National Character.'

" The Council of the Guild of St. Matthew often held its meetings at the hospitable Minor Canon's house in Amen Court. In 1886, after he was established as Rector of St. Nicholas Cole Abbey, where he started such a mass of lecturing, Sunday and week-day, it became impracticable for him to continue lecturing for the Guild. Hitherto only one of the London clergy belonging to the Guild of St. Matthew, the Rev. C. E. Escreet, of St. Andrew's, Stockwell (now Rector of Woolwich), had been established by being beneficed.

" His popularity, which he had set at so low a price by identifying himself with the Guild of St. Matthew, had afterwards to endure the test of a more serious purgatory. The blind

prophets of this present evil world, secular and
religious, saw that none of their predictions had
come to pass. The man whom they had
warned and scolded, who had refused to follow
their counsels, had evidently grown in favour
with men as well as God. His favour had
widened and deepened, instead of declining,
since he had declared that he felt obliged to
be a Socialist because he was a Churchman.
Then the world utterly changed its course: it
began, by the ministry of its so-called 'Priesthood of the Newspaper Press,' to applaud,
photograph, interview, and describe him in all
manner of detail, for the entertainment of its
reading classes and the profit of its shareholding
classes. Henry Shuttleworth was suddenly
raised by the religious press almost to a level
of religious equality with the world's biggest
idols in the Dissenting pulpit, whom I need not
name; he and his work became a prey for the
'personal journalists' in their everlasting hunt
after fresh 'copy.' This was a sort of glory
which had hitherto been sparsely allowed to the
clergy, and it had been restricted to those of his
brethren who were least like him, to clergymen
who had made themselves acceptable to the
world, and had got upon the direct road to
preferment in the Church, by their more or less

undiscerning flatteries of separatists from the Church.

" It was a matter of delight and gratitude to his friends, to see how the Grace of God kept this dear soul as unhurt and unspotted in the midst of the flaming hell of a rare popularity, as he would have been in the purgatory of a persecution.

" The applause that would have ruined many another man never seemed to do him the least hurt. He was aware alike of its worthlessness and its worth. It was of real service to him because he lived for others and knew to what good use he could put this talent. He expended all that he got in praise or pence upon the service of those who were in need of his help. If he had lost his great stock of popularity, he was rich enough in better treasures to have lived without it. So long as he had it (and he retained it to the end), he laid it all out upon the redemption and education of ' Esau.' "

Some interesting letters, belonging to this period, and kindly contributed by the Rev. F. L. Donaldson, may fitly be inserted here.

Writing in December 1876 of a great Nonconformist leader and preacher, the late George Dawson of Birmingham, Shuttleworth says—

F

"I don't think he would wish to be considered 'one of the greatest and most powerful enemies of the Church,' as you call him. He knew his Bible too well for that. And, now that the veil is withdrawn from his eyes, he knows better what the Church is than he did in life. Give him the old prayer of the Catholic Church for the departed—'May he rest in peace.'"

And again, writing of some photographs which were sent him, he says—

> "*Chapter-House, St. Paul's, E C*
>
> "*30 Jan. '77.*

"I am glad to have that of George Dawson and your junior M.P.[1] Though I suppose I agree little enough with either, I always respect intellectual power and independent thought; all the more if it is joined with earnestness in religion, and zeal for the Master's service—even though in my view it may be zeal not according to knowledge."

He felt very strongly indeed upon the "Ritual" agitations, and his opinions have, after five-and-twenty years, a curious appropriateness to quite recent and similar crises. He writes as follows on the occasion of Mr. Gladstone's visit to Birmingham in 1877—

[1] Joseph Chamberlain.

" Chapter-House, St. Paul's, E.C.
"June 18, 1877.

" I wish I had been there to join in the homage, by which Birmingham did more honour to itself than to its object. He is the grandest figure of modern times ; he stands out against the dark background of almost universal want of principle among public men, of political jugglery and time-serving, of a mean and contemptible preference of ' our own interests ' to justice and humanity—a man who is in earnest, a man with a conscience, a Christian statesman, who has dared to brush away with both hands his popularity among two-thirds of the party he once led, rather than stand by in silence, when wrong was done.

" I only wish we had a few such true and brave men upon the bench of Bishops—or even one who feared God more than *The Times !* It is the Bishops who are answerable for the greater part of the scandals which disgrace the Church. They drove out Wesley, and they will drive out us poor High-Church folks if they can. Perhaps you will live to see your Padre a priest of a Free Church. Not that he would leave the English Church ; that would be schism, unless the Church became committed to heresy, and they are but faithless sailors who leave the old ship in the midst of the breakers. But things are coming to such a pass that unless the rulers in Church and State try to govern by other means than tyranny, injustice, and sham law, there will be no resource but Disestablishment."

In the same year he writes—

"My chief fear is that there may be a prosecution at St. Barnabas (Oxford)—that those excellent Christians whose mission seems to be the stirring-up of strife may bribe three drunken tinkers, or other equally well-qualified gentlemen, to put down Ritualism. Well, if so, the Vicar will go to jail. And that fact will be the most effective sermon he could ever preach. More than two-thirds of the householders in the parish have memorialized him to go on as he is doing, churchmen and dissenters alike."

In his opinion the hubbub in the newspapers and in Parliament about *The Priest in Absolution* was in reality an attack upon any restraint of impurity. Though generally he disliked and disapproved of the book, he detected the cant and insincerity of the opposing forces.

"I am a member [1] of the Society of the Holy Cross, and have been for seven years. And I am proud of it. The attack upon us has been simply brutal and unjust to the last degree. I possess, though I had not read, and now do not like, *The Priest in Absolution*. The extracts, however, made from it are most grossly unfair;

---

[1] He afterwards resigned.

I have verified them all. They are misquoted
in almost every instance; the context is invariably suppressed; qualifying and explanatory
matter omitted, strong and repeated cautions
ignored. And the Christian gentlemen who
have made this attack have been pleased
to write and speak as if these 'disgusting
questions' were asked in every case, of every
person, of every age and rank whoever came
to Confession. The book expressly forbids any
such questions, unless, from information received
or from the penitent's own confession, the priest
knows that sin of that kind has been committed.
People are ready enough to *commit* impure
sins. But directly an effort is made to counter-
act the terrible prevalence of impurity in every
form, this cry is raised."

Shuttleworth's work in London soon over-
flowed the Cathedral and its precincts. He
became known as a lecturer, and was soon
brought into conflict with Secularism, which
was then, between 1877 and 1887, in the heyday of its influence. He writes in 1878—

"I am hard at work. Just now, I have a
weekly lecture to working-men, mostly disciples
of Bradlaugh. They listen and are courteous.
But I doubt if argument can convince them.
It is their hearts that want touching, more than
their heads."

He became increasingly involved in these controversies, and he plunged with all his enthusiasm into the fray. The following is a specimen of many letters which he wrote in these years. It indicates the immense and generous trouble he took with comparatively humble folk. He entered with intense earnestness into their difficulties. His letter is written to a youth of eighteen who used to frequent Secularist Halls.

"Your two questions are too wide to be answered satisfactorily within the limits of a letter. But both rest upon an assumption or upon assumptions which I cannot accept. Where in Scripture is the omnipresence of a personal devil asserted? 1. There are more than one evil spirit, but I know not what Bible language ascribes omnipresence to one of them. The fact is that Milton is responsible for the popular or supposed belief as to Satan. And almost all the more specious anti-Christian, or at any rate anti-scriptural, arguments are heavy blows to Calvinism and Protestantism, but do not tell with anything like the same force against the Catholic Faith.

"This point is brought out most vividly by a recent writer, Mallock of Balliol, in the *Contemporary Review.* The whole question of the personality of evil is subtle and profound. I have read something about it, and what seems the strongest argument in its favour to my mind, is perhaps the traces of the working of a *mind*, an active malignant *mind*—in human life and history, and therefore of a person. Have you never seemed to feel yourself that some one else was in the room when you were alone ?

" Believing in the personality of evil myself, I do not think it is an integral portion of Christian faith ; or so clearly revealed as to be certain on one side or the other.

" 2. Your second question rests on a most common misconception—that the word 'prophet' means a foreteller of the future. It is as true to say that the word 'parson' means a man who performs marriages. That is one of his functions undoubtedly, but by no means the sole or the chief, and there are lots of parsons who never do it. The same is true of the prophet in the Old Testament. He was *a revealer of God to man ;* often involving prediction, but not necessarily, and including the functions of preacher, teacher, chorister, musician ; sometimes also those of statesman and poet. Isaiah's poetry has seldom been surpassed, whilst a recent infidel writer has been obliged to admit that the finest poem in the literature of the world is the 104th Psalm. Is not the word psalmist rather near the idea of poet ? Hebrew poetry was not rhyming or rhythmical, it consisted of parallelisms, of which the Old Testament books are full, and a good example of which is the poetical prophecy of Balaam.

"As to the 'evil spirit from the Lord.' It is said of Saul in the Book of Samuel. It rather touches our first question. But there are three canons of Old Testament criticism you must not leave out of sight—

"(1) Every sentiment in a book written by inspiration is not inspired.

"(2) Every action of inspired men was not done by inspiration.

"(3) The Hebrew idiom, or rather the genius of Hebrew literature, speaks of God doing that which He *allowed* to be done.

"The inspiration of the Bible only covers the message its writers were empowered to deliver, and does not touch matter of science and history.

"Of course this is not the Calvinistic view. I have read Strauss, Bradlaugh, and many unbelieving writers; and the English infidels all seem to argue as if they took Calvinism, or at least Protestantism, to be synonymous with Christianity. Therefore they are generally wide of *my* faith.

"Belief in God is far too great a question to enter upon here. But it seems to me to follow from belief in man and in nature. How otherwise account for the universal sense of responsibility and the idea of duty?—to say nothing of conscience, design, etc. 'Every child is born an atheist,' says Mr. Bradlaugh; if so, atheism must have existed before theism, and powerful indeed must be the evidence which has so changed the conditions of the whole human race, that only the lowest and most brutish African tribes, of all men, know no God. If all children are atheists, few men are ; and it would seem to follow logically that atheism is childish. Bacon says, 'a little knowledge inclineth men's minds to atheism ; but depth in philosophy bringeth men's minds close to religion.' "

I have given this letter in full as an instance of the immense and painstaking trouble which he took with his correspondence, and with his endeavour to commend the Faith to those who are without. Here is another of the same type—

" You say, you are 'unbaptized, unconfirmed, and irreligious.' I could pardon you the first two much more readily than the last, this not being ashamed to own it, in an off-hand kind of way, which pains me so much. Try and see, that just as a man can never command, who has never learnt to obey, so a man who has never been sorry for sin, can never be a good man ; unless, of course, he has never sinned. Read the last sentence at the beginning of morning and evening prayer, in our Prayer-book."

His work among Secularists was wonderful. He did more than any other person in England during 1880–1890 to take the heart out of the

Secularist movement, on its anti-Christian side.
He lectured incessantly and wrote innumerable
letters and articles. This aspect of his work
was thus described in a sermon preached after
his death—

"Think of his noble work amongst the
Secularists of London, his splendid witness to
the faith amongst them. There was scarce a
Hall frequented by these Secularists in which
his voice has not been heard, pleading with them
for the Faith, scarcely a man or woman, within
those circles, who, if still unconvinced, was not
softened in spirit, moved in their affections by
the constraining witness which he bore for
Christ amongst them. Think of him later, when
the movement of 'Secularism' was passing
into 'Socialism,' equally in earnest to claim for
Christ any earnest social effort which seemed to
strengthen and deepen the Brotherhood of Man."

Speaking of unity in religion as necessary
to the highest form of friendship, he writes in
1878—

"I doubt whether friendship and love can
be of the highest order when there is not unity
of heart upon the things that are dearest to one
or both."

Writing in 1880 to a younger friend, he says—

"I am sure that cold and unassisted argument
will never make you a Christian, or anything
else except a wanderer and a sceptic, who
wavers between one thing and another, and ends
by believing none—a cynic of the type you and
I agree in dreading and disliking. All that
argument can do for you is to show you that the
Christian Faith is not harder to believe than
any other system ; is, I think, far easier. *Then*
comes in the answer which it, and it only, gives
to those cravings of heart and soul which you
have felt. Only Jesus of Nazareth can satisfy
them ; only He, of all earth's teachers, even
dared to promise *rest* to His followers, and
that because He alone could give it. . . . I pray
daily that in His own time you may know that
rest."

To a man preparing for Holy Orders he
writes—

"Of all callings none is like that of the
priest for greatness and enthusiasm. It has
its disappointments and heart-aches of course,
but there is that which outweighs them all."

And again—

"You will be a better priest, be sure, for
having known trouble, anxiety, and disappoint-
ment now. Take care that while it opens
your eyes to the bitter fact of the prevalence
of evil, it does not weaken your power of

sympathy with those in sorrow, or destroy your belief in the final victory of right.

"Your loneliness is meant, I think, to drive you to our Lord as a real, living Person, Who knows and loves you, and follows each step of your life. Make a friend of Him."

The following testimony from a well-known layman may be suitably inserted in this place—

"When Shuttleworth came to London in 1876, he attracted a good deal of attention, and did something in the City at least to stir up the enthusiasm of the young laymen. It was something new to have anybody connected with St. Paul's Cathedral who would look upon young clerks and young warehousemen in the City as being worth attention, and as possessing material which might be used for the good of the Church and the Commonwealth. Those were glorious days. The young Churchmen in the City were all alive, the City Branch of the E.C.U. was something worth knowing, and one used to hear a good deal about Shuttleworth ; the practice of calling him 'Canon' began with those City lads, and it stuck to him ever since.

"The first time I heard him preach was when he took the Three Hours' Service on Good Friday in 1878. A disturbance was expected, and had been carefully prepared by the Protestant organizers. Shuttleworth was really splendid; the way in which so young a man held that huge congregation was very fine; the circumstances were trying, the date indicates that, and the occasion was certainly a great one. His words rang in my ears for many months afterwards.

"Soon after that I got to know him. At that time there were troubles in the S.S C.,[1] and some of the younger clergy were inclined to say, and did say, very hard things of Shuttleworth; that he had become a Universalist, etc., etc. There is no doubt that his views were changing, but it was impossible not to like him, and although one felt sorry he was drifting away from the old lines, nevertheless, one retained respect for him on account of his work, and the need there seemed to be for pushing Catholic principles along unknown and hitherto untrodden paths. Any man who did that would be sure to suffer to some extent in the estimation of his fellows; it was so with Shuttleworth.

"I got to know Shuttleworth through the Church and Stage Guild, and the Guild of St. Matthew. The Church and Stage Guild used to have its little services in the Crypt of St.

[1] The Society of the Holy Cross, designed to deepen the spiritual life of clergymen.

Paul's, and the Guild of St. Matthew was then hotly engaged in dealing with the old Bradlaugh Secularism, which was mainly a revolt from Calvinism. Touching Shuttleworth's connexion with things theatrical, I very well remember the praise which was given to an article which he wrote in the *Church Reformer*, in February 1884, on the play at the Princess's, called *Claudian*.

" The Guild of St. Matthew, and its lecturers, in the very front rank of whom should be placed Shuttleworth and Headlam, helped to destroy Secularism, although, perhaps, the Guild did not represent the only force working against it. The rise of the Socialist movement could not fail to affect Mr. Bradlaugh's movement, and did in the end help to destroy it.

" I accompanied Shuttleworth on several occasions to lectures in Secularist Halls. There was one in Walworth which I remember very well. It was, indeed, trying to have to go and debate with those fellows, and hear the shocking things they said of our Lord and His Blessed Mother. Shuttleworth was never at a loss for a telling reply, but he kept his temper most admirably, so well indeed, that I remember on one occasion, at that very Walworth Hall, those responsible for the place plainly showed that they felt ashamed of the blasphemies of some amongst the audience. I have always felt that I owed much to Shuttleworth in the way of learning how to deal with people of this sort

"In the summer of 1887 I went with Shuttleworth to address the English Church Union at Norwich; our theme was the Church in relation to Democracy; the meetings were most interesting, and what we said was extremely well received, although there had been some recent local excitement which had ended in the imprisonment of two socialists in Norwich Castle.

"In 1888 the Social question had reached a point when, as Sydney Webb, the Fabian, said, 'even the Bishops believed and trembled.' The Guild of St. Matthew presented a memorial to the Conference of Bishops then assembled at Lambeth. I was one of the Signatories, and helped to draw up the document; it led to what was regarded as a satisfactory and remarkable pronouncement on the part of the Bishops, and Thorold, Bishop of Rochester, that year preached the anniversary sermon for the Guild in the Church of St. John the Evangelist, Waterloo Road.

"Shuttleworth then determined that he would have a page of notes dealing with social questions in his magazine. That magazine had qualities not generally to be found in such publications, and he asked me to write the notes month by month; I did so for several years.

"No man could possibly have carried on the work that Shuttleworth did without getting wounded. Reviewing his career, I am inclined to think that his very best work was that in which he fought against the Secularism of the Seventies, and, as far as I am able to judge, he did this without sacrificing one scrap of vital Christian principle. Mrs. Besant and Mr. Herbert Burrows ought to be able to bear ungrudging and generous testimony to Shuttleworth's fidelity to his own principles in this struggle.

"I have a theory that Priests who are attracted by, and have much to do with, music lose in time that sense of proportion which it is so desirable to preserve in all of us, most of all in the clergy. If I am right, Shuttleworth may have been influenced in this way. But surely he was a man to whom much might be forgiven. He had courage; in days when to be a Liberal involved the risk of being called an Atheist, or of being denounced as a person to be avoided for making 'common cause with Atheists,' he was a Liberal. He was just; although he fought the Secularists, he helped them when they were unjustly assailed by prosecutions under the obsolete and foolish Blasphemy Laws."

Here is an interesting touch of portraiture by the Rev. F. L. Donaldson—

"*His power of romance* was enormous. He had the rare faculty of idealism, both of people and of things, which, though it sometimes led him astray, made one of the most potent elements for good in his character and work. He invested things with a kind of halo, and then proceeded to pray and work accordingly. This enabled him to 'go on long after others had given up.' For instance, in his lectures to Secularists he idealized his audience. To him they were all 'seekers after truth,' whereas, in fact, while there were some truth-seekers amongst them, the majority came to hear a good lecture and to argue. But he idealized *all*, and no doubt had power with them according.

"'We must never,' he said to me after a mission in the back streets of Soho, 'patronize the working-men; we must talk to them as to equals, and not as superiors to inferiors.' One secret of his success in these unconventional

G

circles lay in the readiness with which he adapted his sympathies to the brethren around him. He made himself one with them. In the best sense of the words he 'made himself all things to all men, if by any means he might save some.'"

Meanwhile, on the 16th October, 1878, Shuttleworth had been married to Mary, daughter of Dr. Fuller, a well-known physician at Shoreham. The blessings of the man who hath his quiver full of them were not denied him, and he was naturally anxious for a more permanent and independent post than that of a Minor Canon.

In 1880 he had some thoughts of applying for a Lectureship at one of the City churches; and the following letter is so characteristic of the man, and sheds so clear a light upon the struggles of his bright-seeming life, that it must be reproduced in its entirety—

"*February* 16, 1880.

"Your note certainly annoyed me; but not by what you said about my sermon so much as the suggestion that, were I a Mason, I should have a better chance of the Lectureship. I can hardly tell you how much I hate the notion of owing any preferment to such influence. I want a City Lectureship for two reasons: first, I am a poor man and should be glad of the money; and next, I desire some recognized position as a preacher. At present, including crypt-lectures, I preach perhaps twelve times in a year in St. Paul's, and, if I never preached elsewhere, I should lose my extempore power, such as it is, and my voice would be seldom heard. I dislike running all over London to preach: and the Chapter dislike my doing so. So I wish for a Lectureship. But I will lick the boots of no City magnate to get that, or anything else. I wish to owe any position I may have to the fact that I am fit to hold it; and to no back-stairs influence. I hate the City for the very reason that there is so much of this grovelling on the one hand, and patronizing on the other. I will not grovel, and I will not be patronized by Masons, or tallow-chandlers, or swindling City millionaires. If they like to offer me a post which I am able worthily to fulfill, and to offer it like gentlemen to a gentleman, I will take it and thank them for it. I am not ashamed of letting it be known that I want a Lectureship, or of telling any one my reasons for wanting it. I should be ashamed of holding such an office if I had obtained it because I was a Freemason, or because I happened to know some fussy Jack-in-office of a trustee."

It needs no great knowledge of Cathedrals and Dignitaries—their inveterate conservatism and their suffocating respectability—to divine that such methods as those which Shuttleworth pursued when Minor Canon of St. Paul's would render him an object of profound suspicion in decanal and canonical eyes. Perhaps if he had figured on Conservative platforms, spouted for Church and State, and rent the heavens with denunciations of Socialism, the authorities might have waived their objection to the intervention of their fiery colleague in public and secular affairs. But, things being as they were, it soon became apparent that his room would be more valued than his company; and to offer him one of the Chapter's livings was the easiest and most decent way of evicting the unruly member.

Accordingly, in November 1883, he was presented by the Dean and Chapter to the Rectory of St. Nicholas Cole Abbey, in Queen Victoria Street. Henceforward his Socialism, his Secularism, and his Eclecticism were to be manifested in another sphere, and there can be very little doubt that "Egypt was glad at their departing."

As to the impression which Shuttleworth left upon the minds of the Dean and Chapter, the Rev. Henry Scott Holland, who became a Canon of St. Paul's in 1884, writes thus: "I was not here at St. Paul's with him, and have therefore no personal recollections. When I arrived here, I found rather the head-shakings of those who were very fond of him over his 'dreadful Socialism.' They all spoke a little sadly, as if he had 'gone wrong,' but of course this only amused me."

At this point I may insert an interesting note by the Rev. Thomas Hancock—

"I owed to Shuttleworth my restitution to the exercise of the ministry which I had received from the Lord, from which I had for years been excluded, save in a few parishes whose priests were Socialists. I was in my fifty-second year, and had little prospect of recovering it. One night in November 1883, after one of our clerical suppers, Henry Shuttleworth said: 'Hancock, can you give me five minutes? The Chapter of St. Paul's have offered me the rectory of St. Nicholas Cole Abbey · I find there is a lecture-ship attached to it. If the Bishop of London will license you, will you take it?' I cannot forget that night. He had given my youth back again to me, and re-opened the doors of the House of the Lord to one of His ejected priests, that he might go in again and find his place in it. I went home astounded, feeling as if a new age had come. To none of the clergy of our time do I owe such a debt as I do to Henry Shuttleworth. For he it was who gave back to me in 1884, all that Bishop Wilberforce had given me by my ordination nearly a quarter of a century before."

The church of St. Nicholas Cole Abbey is of very ancient foundation. The first rector, Thomas de Isham, was appointed in 1319. The present edifice was built by Sir Christopher Wren in 1677, at a cost of £5042 ; the former building having been destroyed in the great fire of London. It is the parish church of six parishes—St. Nicholas Cole Abbey, St. Mary Somerset, St. Nicholas Olave, St. Mary Mounthaw, St. Benet Paul's Wharf, and St. Peter Paul's Wharf. Shuttleworth used sometimes to relate the circumstances under which he first saw the church. "I was at that time on the staff of the Cathedral, and I came here for the then curate, Mr. Fox Taylor. It was the custom for the bell to be rung on Thursdays at midday, and a clergyman 'looked in.' If anybody was in the church I don't know what happened. But as a rule you 'looked in' and went away again. At least, that is what I did, acting upon instructions. The place was in excellent order and scrupulously clean, but dreary beyond description, with a smell of window-open-once-a-month. I little thought as I looked round the empty sanctuary that I should be called to minister there during the best years of my life."

The new Rector "read himself in" on Sunday morning, the 18th January, 1884. Recalling the event in 1899, he writes—

"Looking at an old scrap-book I observe that one of the newspaper scribes who attended this function was good enough to say that I accomplished the rare feat of making the Thirty-Nine Articles interesting. I find myself wondering, fifteen years after, how in the world I could have managed that. Indeed, a clergyman who had seen the newspaper paragraph, and was about to read himself in, solemnly wrote to me to ask how it was done—there lives no record of reply."

Shuttleworth entered on his new sphere of work with all the vigour of manhood—he was then thirty-three years of age—and with a knowledge and experience of human beings, and especially of young men, which few clergymen acquire in a long lifetime.

What was the problem before him?—"A City church, swept and garnished indeed, but also empty." What could be done with it? He solved the problem by making the empty church a full church, the centre of a vigorous life and of manifold activities in the service of

God and the fellowship of Man.   He restored
the early Celebration of Holy Communion.
He instituted a choral Eucharist at midday, in
place of the service which in so many other
churches is but "glorified mattins," and, as has
been lately remarked, "through all changes of
opinion, he maintained the Mass as the principal
Service at his church."   He was assisted by
an able organist and a mixed choir of men
and women, which rendered the works of the
great Church composers with dignity and devotion, and which, in an artistic sense, has rarely
been surpassed in any English church.   This
Service was highly valued and appreciated by
the faithful few.   It never drew large congregations, except on the great Festivals, and this
was, to the end, always a matter of disappoint-
ment and regret to the Rector.   The most
popular service at St. Nicholas was the seven
o'clock Evensong.   This was always crowded to
excess.   It was most difficult to find accommodation for the crowds that came ; and very many
had to go away, time after time, because there
was no room for them, sitting or standing, in
the church.   It was not a cathedral service,
but congregational—choral, with plain Anglican
chants and hymns.   There was no anthem,
though a Service of Song rendered by the choir

and conducted by the Rector, occasionally followed the service. The large congregation was mainly conspicuous for its youthful element—in fact St. Nicholas Cole Abbey earned the title of being "a young man's church." The heartiness of the responses, the singing of the chants and hymns, and above all, the true teaching, persuasive eloquence and power of the Rector's preaching, will never be forgotten by those who were privileged to work under and worship with him.

A very important feature in the life of St. Nicholas was the Sunday afternoon Lecture and Oratorio. Shuttleworth had often felt on Sunday afternoons that the closed doors of the church were a standing reproach to him. A paragraph in the *Pall Mall Gazette* set him dreaming upon the thought of a day when each Sunday afternoon a great Oratorio, with full orchestra, should be given in St. Paul's. He could not do that at St. Nicholas, though only from lack of funds; but he thought he might do something towards it. The choir fell into the idea with never-failing readiness. But he felt he could not lay so heavy a burden upon them as an Oratorio every Sunday would mean. So he arranged for an Oratorio every third or fourth Sunday, and in intermediate

Sundays for a Lecture, treating of some general
subject from the point of view of Christian
theology. He did not think it necessary to
defend or apologize for such an undertaking.
Lectures or "Conferences" of this sort were no
novelties· they interfered with no other requirements or services : they met the needs of many
who never went to hear sermons, and a City
church, with few parochial claims, seemed to
be the best place for the experiment. It was
entirely successful; the Lectures were of a high
order, as may be judged from the names of
the lecturers. Eminent clergymen, like Bishop
Creighton, Bishop Winnington-Ingram, Bishop
Barry, Bishop Gore, Dean Farrar, Canon Scott
Holland, Canon Barnett, Archdeacon Sinclair,
and others, all most kindly gave their help.
Each Lecture was given apart from any service
except the "Bidding Prayer" before and a
collect after, and a hymn ; a short Organ-recital,
with one or two sacred songs, preceded and
followed the Lecture with excellent effect. The
subjects embraced such burning questions as
Church Reform, Some Aspects of Disestablishment, Social Repentance, the Christian Ideal of
Marriage, the Place of Amusement in Earnest
Life, Hymns and Hymn-tunes, with illustrations : the great Church composers, from Pales-

trina and his precursors to Purcell, Goss, and
Henry Smart: Sacred Art and great Christian
Painters ; the religious teaching of such leaders
of thought as Browning, Tennyson, Matthew
Arnold, and John Ruskin. In fact, almost all
the subjects of interest in the religious world
or bearing on the cultivation of the Christian
character, were discussed in these memorable
Lectures.   The congregations were always
good, and on the occasions when an Oratorio
or musical recital was given, the church was
filled to overflowing.

An article on "Sunday Music in the City" in
the *Daily Telegraph*, on the 26th September,
1887, describes how "Many churches stand
around Queen Victoria Street, but yesterday
the saunterer in that locality on Sunday afternoon may have observed that they were all shut.
In that case he was probably astonished to
hear from St. Nicholas the sound of organ and
voices uplifted lustily in 'anthem clear.' Of
course he entered to satisfy himself about such
a phenomenon, and this is what he saw: a
rectangular interior of a type common in the
City, made beautiful by carved oak and tasteful
decoration ; at the east end a surpliced choir,
strengthened by many ladies and conducted by
a clergyman who wields the baton like an

adept; and all over the church a packed, orderly, and attentive crowd, scores of whom are content to stand for lack of seats. Can this be a church in the forsaken City, where, as we often hear, it is so difficult to gather a congregation on Sundays? Indeed it is. But our imagined visitor does not long wonder at the throng gathered there in a place of worship that might easily be lost among so many. The choir of about forty voices is busy, under the Rector's guidance, in performing Samuel Sebastian Wesley's anthem, 'The Wilderness and the solitary place shall be made glad for them,' and very worthily do conductor, organist, and singers enter into the spirit of that magnificent example of English Church music—a composition which revives in our day the genius of the masters who generations ago gave us so precious a legacy of sacred art."

The Rector of St. Nicholas believed that music could preach a powerful sermon and was often able to reach and move those who were untouched by spoken addresses. The selection of music performed at St. Nicholas during the years when these Oratorios were conducted is too long to enumerate. Sufficient to recall Spohr's 'Last Judgment' and 'Calvary,' Mozart's 'Requiem,' Handel's 'Messiah,'

Haydn's 'Creation,' Mendelssohn's 'Hymn of Praise,' 'Elijah,' and 'St. Paul,' Gounod's 'Redemption' and 'Gallia,' Sterndale Bennett's 'Woman of Samaria,' Stainer's 'Daughter of Jairus,' and Sullivan's 'Light of the World,' 'Prodigal Son,' and the 'Golden Legend.' But in course of time these musical services ceased to attract the very large congregations they did at first and for some years afterwards. Writing on the subject to a member of his Church Council on the 20th November, 1896, Shuttleworth said—

"No musician could say with truth that the rendering of our musical services has degenerated—the exact contrary is the fact. The attendance has decreased; and the cause is to my mind obvious. We are not now alone in the field—there is excellent Sunday music at Queen's Hall, Albert Hall, South Place, and a dozen other churches, which as usual have copied us. But there are no Lectures anywhere like ours. I myself called attention to the falling off of the afternoon—not the evening— Oratorio congregations at the beginning of 1895, in the February magazine and at the Church Council. The remedy would be to engage a small orchestra, to advertise largely and paragraph the newspapers freely; and to engage 'star-singers.' The last I will never stoop to do, having always gone on the

Bayreuth principle that the star-system is ruin to real art; the two first are quite possible if the money *is* forthcoming."

Shuttleworth spared no effort to make St. Nicholas useful during the week. The church was always open for private devotion and meditation. A careful selection of about a hundred books were arranged on shelves at the west end of the church for the benefit of any who cared to make use of them, and very many availed themselves of this privilege. Probably the most successful attempt to make the church useful on week-days was the Organ Recital on Tuesday evening. Commenting upon these, the *City Press* of the 15th December, 1897, said : " The programme of music played at the usual organ recital yesterday in St. Nicholas Cole Abbey contained the significant announcement that this was the sixth hundred and thirty-fifth recital. For nearly fourteen years during the present Rector's incumbency, these recitals have continued with scarcely a break, except during the holiday month of August, and from the first they have been regularly attended, week by week, by about a hundred and fifty to two hundred persons, mostly men. When they began, no other City church provided such services, except on rare occasions.

Now they are a regular institution in many churches. Mr. Shuttleworth, as usual, led the way; but at least an equal measure of credit is due to the brilliant young organist, Mr. Ralph Norris, whom he brought as a boy from Oxford, and who has fully justified his choice!"

Week-day services, in the ordinary sense, were never fully appreciated at St. Nicholas. The Rector, assisted by his various curates, made several attempts, from time to time, at mid-day and in the evening, to make the church useful in this respect; but, except during the seasons of Advent and Lent, the congregations were always small. In the early days before there was any Parish-Room or other place of meeting than the church, Lectures were given on Thursday evenings, on various subjects of universal interest The course on Tennyson's 'In Memoriam' will long be remembered.

Shuttleworth was by no means forgetful of the social life of his people. In his pastoral address of January 1885, he said: "We need to know each other better, and I hope to find some means of bringing this about." During 1886 the desirable object was to a certain extent attained by means of social gatherings of various kinds, but chiefly perhaps by the successful "Cinderella Dances" arranged by the Entertainment Committee of the Church Council. Country rambles in the summer months and a cricket and tennis club were started with every success. Of course the Rector of St. Nicholas got into trouble with *The Rock* and *The English Churchman*. But, as he explained, "We ought to recognize the fact that such views of our work are widely held. We are thought to be 'secularizing' holy things; to be making terms with the world; to be of the number of advertising ecclesiastical quacks who attract attention by 'extraordinary novelties.' As to the two former charges, I have simply to say that when the objectors will give me a reasonable explanation of the difference between things sacred and things secular, I shall be prepared to meet them. Meanwhile, I believe, with the Archbishop of Canterbury (Dr. Benson), that 'to the Church, nothing is secular but what is sinful.' The whole of human life is sanctified by the Incarnation of our Lord; even its recreations. The world, in its bad sense, does not mean our fellow-men, or the beauty and joy and pleasant intercourse of life, or the constituted order of civil society. It means devotion to outward things, such as money, or party, or respectability, to the exclusion of unseen ideas, such as honour, truth and brotherhood. As to the third point, I can only meet it with a categorical negative. I covet no reputation so little as that of a clerical sensation-monger, and I may frankly confess that various plans are yet unborn from sheer fear of their being supposed to be some new dodge for getting people to church or for putting myself *en évidence*."

The Rector of St. Nicholas was, of course, more the Minister of a Congregation than a Parish Priest. It was in the year 1886 that anything like regular organization was first attempted. The bond of neighbourhood which binds fellow-parishioners or close neighbours to one another was lacking; and other means had to be devised for supplying its place. The first step was the enrolment of regular members of the congregation in a Register; and the second was the election of a Council or Committee by all who were thus enrolled. The qualification for registered membership was regular attendance at the services of St. Nicholas Cole Abbey. Members received a card of Membership, which was renewed each year if desired. The bulk of the congregation

H

did not come from the parish ; but this may be said of other congregations besides St. Nicholas. For, as Shuttleworth used to say, " However we may regret it, the fact is that the old feeling which kept Englishmen to their own parish church is dead, at least in large towns. Whether we like it or not people will go to the church they prefer. It is really a kind of protest against the loss of their ancient right to elect their own parish priest. They practically elect their pastor now by going away from their parish church if they choose." St. Nicholas Cole Abbey met the needs of a large number of people, the great majority of whom lived, or were employed in the City of London. The Church Council was an experiment, and most fully justified itself. Its objects were—

A. To advise with the Rector upon all matters of interest to the congregation and in regard to the Services of the Church.
B. To assist the clergy in carrying out the various works undertaken from time to time in connexion with St. Nicholas.

The Council consisted of—

Ex-officio Members.

  A. The Rector, as President, and the licensed clergy.

B. Any Churchwardens, as Vestry clerks, of the united parishes who might signify their wish to serve.

Elected Members.

A. Fifteen members to be elected by the Registered Members of the congregation.

B. Two members to be elected annually by the members, from among their own number, of any recognized society in connexion with the Church of St. Nicholas.

New candidates were required to be nominated in writing by the Registered Members of the congregation, such nominations to be sent to the Rector and posted in the church porch at least one month before the annual meeting of the congregation. One-third of the elected members from the congegation retired annually, being eligible for re-election, and if more candidates were nominated than there were vacancies, a ballot was taken, and a voting paper was sent to every Registered Member of the congregation. The Council did not, of course, interfere with legal matters, which belonged to the Vestry, nor did it assume any right of government or control over the church. The Church Council of St. Nicholas Cole Abbey met eight times in the year to consult, to advise and to organize. The discussions at its meetings were business-like and suggestive. The Council appointed sub-committees to arrange such matters as the decoration of the church, entertainments and social functions, and more particularly, finance. The Rector was thus brought very much into touch with his people, and it gave the congregation full opportunity of making its wants and feelings known to the Rector. A General Meeting of the Registered Members of the congregation was held in the church at the beginning of each year, when a report and statement of the Offertory-account was submitted on behalf of the Council. The reports of the various Societies were also read. A discussion followed on some one or more subjects in connexion with the church, its services or its work, at which members were invited to freely express their opinions. A pastoral address was delivered by the Rector at the end of the meeting. These pastoral addresses were not to outsiders, but, as he used to explain, to "the inner circle of St. Nicholas Cole Abbey." They gave the Rector a unique opportunity. "I can speak to you with a directness impossible at any other time: since I have you here by yourselves and need not fear that outsiders may misunderstand what I say" On Septuagesima Sunday 1890, he said : "When first we came to St. Nicholas some of the methods we adopted were regarded as new, as even dangerous; and we have had to take our share of the prejudice and abuse which is the lot of those who venture on comparatively untrodden ways, especially in ecclesiastical regions. There are, you know, three stages through which every new ideal or fresh method has to pass in England. The first, when everybody laughs at it and says, ' It is impossible;' the second, when everybody frowns and says, ' It is against the Bible;' the third, when everybody smiles and says, 'We knew that before.' We at St. Nicholas have now reached the third stage. The first we have long since left behind. Nobody doubts now that it is possible to turn a deserted City church to some better use than destruction. Out of the second we have not entirely passed; there are still not a few who think we are unscriptural, improper persons, who ought to be 'put down.' But that we have advanced into the third stage is surely plain, for our 'new and dangerous' methods are being adopted on all sides. We began organ recitals on week-days—and we were secularizing a sacred building. We did not look upon stage-folk as unfit to associate with us : and we were 'shaking hands with the world.' We had Sunday Oratorios and Sunday Lectures in church, and we were turning God's house into a concert-room or a theatre. We had dances now and then, when we wanted to amuse ourselves : and no imprecation was too sulphurous, no lie too absurd but it would do for the folks who could thus profane the 'eve of the Sabbath '—a novel holy day, unknown to Christendom until now. Well, as was said, some of these our iniquities are still in the stage of 'against the Bible.' But everybody now has organ recitals as a matter of course. Sunday Oratorios and Sunday Lectures increase and multiply. An actor is the favoured guest and teacher of a Church Congress, and 'Choir Cinderellas,' though myths at St. Nicholas, are realities in many a London church school-room. In fact the necessity of wholesome recreation and of healthy social life has become a common-place ; and the value of music, as a method of preaching and as a form of prayer, is recognized on all hands. Everybody is saying, 'We knew that before.'"

On a subsequent occasion Shuttleworth took, as the subject of his pastoral address : " Some of the Ways and Methods in which a Congregation can help their Pastor." This was a very powerful address. He said: "It is impossible for any clergyman, whether a Parish Priest like most of us, or whether the minister of a congregation such as circumstances have made me, to stand by himself. Even the strongest man cannot do his work alone, and if he attempts it, or is driven into it, he will become either a recluse or a cipher; or more probably he will break down. He must have the help— the conscious, active, sustained help—of his people." He had lately been reading a remarkable sermon by Dr. Dale, the "Nonconformist Bishop of Birmingham," as he was sometimes called, and that gave point and clearness to thoughts that had been long in his mind. He said—

"1. You have to do your part in the worship of this church."

He impressed upon his people that the services of our English Church are deliberately congregational, and appealed to them to exercise the priesthood of the Christian people, which was their privilege and their right. He pointed out that it made all the difference to the light and warmth of our worship whether the people are concentrated heart and mind upon it, or whether they are there merely to listen or to stare, contributing little or nothing to the common devotion.

" 2. You have to do your part in the teaching. ' People often forget,' truly says Dr. Dale, ' that it takes two to make an effective sermon. the preacher and the hearer.' "

He goes on to recall an old but excellent story of a preacher to whom some well-meaning friend praised inordinately the sermons of olden days. " Ah, sir, there were great preachers then." " Yes," replied the minister, " and there were great hearers then." Congregations do much to make the preachers what they are.

" 3. You can help your clergyman in his pastoral work." The Rector said : " You can make this congregation a real society of Christian people : you can make it a society to which it is a happiness to belong : help me to make our fellowship a reality ; a true Brotherhood in Christ."

He urged them to receive strangers with courtesy and kindness ; and to take, if possible, some interest in one or another of the societies connected with the church.

" 4 Finally, help your clergyman by sometimes allowing him to see some result of his work."

He pointed out that the best of men will become discouraged if they see no result of their work. "A little practical sympathy, an answer to an appeal; some evidence of earnestness, of readiness to take trouble, of thoughtfulness, of affection, of resolve, some sign of increased devotion to the cause of God, to the Person of our Lord, to the service of man—these things help and encourage a pastor more than people know, just as their absence dispirits and disheartens him more than people suspect."

The societies in connexion with St Nicholas Cole Abbey were all, under the Rector's guidance, full of activity and of usefulness. The Guild of SS. Mary and Nicholas directed its energies to the development of the devotional life of its members, especially through the Holy Communion, and to promoting the intellectual side of Christian life by means of Bible Classes, discussions and the like. Its rules were very simple: and any communicant of the English Church being a Registered Member of the congregation of St. Nicholas was eligible for membership. It provided for the service of the Altar; and the artistic decoration in what may be termed the chancel is a memorial of its existence and was paid for out of its funds. The Flower Fund was an endeavour to express that spiritual instinct which would offer up the best and the most beautiful in God's service ; and also to minister to the æsthetic side of our worship. The Ladies' Working Society represented the practical efforts of the congregation to help others.   Much quiet work of the most useful kind was done.   The Society met twice monthly at the Rectory ; and, besides spending pleasant evenings together, made numerous articles of clothing.   These garments were sold to the poor at half the cost price.   Those who received them were members of Clothing-Clubs in Clerkenwell and elsewhere, carried on in the name of St. Nicholas.   Connected with this work was an endeavour to help the children attending certain Board Schools.   Breakfasts and dinners were given to the children, about one hundred and fifty each week in the winter months : and an entertainment at Christmas to as many as funds would allow, when the toys, dolls, books, etc., kindly sent by members of the congregation were distributed.   This branch of the work at St. Nicholas was both successful and useful in no common degree. The Rector said—

" The temptation to a congregation like ours is that we should rest content with our bright services in Church and our pleasant gatherings elsewhere and take a merely dilettante interest in the great question of our time, the abolition of poverty. I am far from dreaming that what we can do at Clerkenwell is likely to effect much towards that end, or that helping a few of the poor is the same thing as abolishing poverty. But no Christian is doing his duty unless, while he strives against the causes which produce poverty, he also does something to relieve the poor. Each can give service if not money, and this work of ours affords us all an opportunity. It is mainly done by women. Let our men help them: they can soon find out how if they will enquire."

The great difficulty with which Shuttleworth had to contend in the early years of his ministry was the want of a Hall or Parish-Room. It hampered him at every turn, and threatened to starve and cramp all his work. No school-room was available. The rents in the City are so gigantic that a room or rooms of sufficient size for the purpose could not be hired except at a very heavy rental. The adjoining parish had a delightful little Parish-Room which was seldom used. He tried several times to obtain the use of it, but though the church-wardens and trustees were willing, the then

Rector declined to lend it for "secular" purposes. The grapes being thus sour, Mr.
Shuttleworth took refuge in the not very con-
soling reflection that the room in question was
"rather small." In 1889 a circular was issued,
stating that the Church of St. Nicholas Cole
Abbey, was attended by large numbers of
young men employed in warehouses and other
places of business in the City, and that the
work done among them by the Rector was
gaining in appreciation and acceptance. Shuttleworth felt that his work had now reached a
point when it must languish and starve, unless
he could provide rooms for classes, lectures,
meetings and social gatherings, so as to form
a centre for the various organizations of a
well-worked church. In an ordinary parish
this would be comparatively easy ; but in the
case of St. Nicholas ,there was no available
room of any kind, and the resources of the
Rectory had been severely taxed in an endeavour to meet the growing need. Two floors
of a warehouse close to the church were taken:
and a thousand pounds was asked to cover
the cost of furnishing, alterations, etc., and
especially to meet the rent for the next three
years. The Rector guaranteed to make the
rooms pay their own working expenses, if the

rent and the first cost could be found from outside. It was intended that the rooms should include—

(*a*) A lecture-room and class-room,

(*b*) A library,

(*c*) A smoking-room for men,

(*d*) A large room available for concerts or social gatherings, which when not so employed should be used as a common room, with books, papers, cards, chess, etc.

It was hoped that the rooms would thus provide the advantages of a Club, with opportunities for culture, amusement, and for that social intercourse in which the ordinary life of young men and women engaged in the City is sadly lacking. No religious test was to be imposed upon those using the rooms, but the work was to be carried on in a religious spirit and in connexion with the Church of St. Nicholas. In October 1889 Shuttleworth wrote—

" The great event of the hour is the opening of the St. Nicholas Club and Parish-Rooms at 81A Queen Victoria Street. They are later in the field than I had hoped ; and we shall hardly get into working order at once. Things must grow. Still it is a great matter to have got the rooms at all ; indeed, I look upon them as the most important event of my work here."

The social life of St. Nicholas Cole Abbey from henceforth became incorporated with the Club; and how the Club developed, and in course of time raised a building of its own, called, at the unanimous request of the members, by its Founder's name, will be described in another part of this memoir.

The *St. Nicholas Cole Abbey Monthly Magazine* was a publication that may be regarded as unique of its kind. At first *On Guard*, the organ of the Young Men's Friendly Society, with which Mr. Shuttleworth was connected, was adopted as a Parish Magazine, and afterwards the *Church Reformer* took its place. But in April 1886 the magazine in its permanent form appeared, and came out regularly every month until April 1900. It was edited by the Rector, and was " all our own," as he said. It contained the usual Church notices; several short paragraphs under the heading of " In the Church Porch," from Mr. Shuttleworth's pen, dealing with matters in connexion with the church and of general interest. Letters to the Editor were received with pleasure, read with mingled feelings, and printed with discretion. It likewise contained the substance of sermons and lectures delivered at St. Nicholas and elsewhere; papers on " Our

Parish Churches"; Reviews of books, Notes
from City Houses, and Theatrical Letters;
papers on Christian Socialism, short stories,
"St. Nicholas Tales," and others; and reports of
all the Parochial Societies, and a record of all
the events in connexion with the church and
club. Without doubt the motive power of
this spiritual organization, in the midst of the
vast City of London, was the personality of
Shuttleworth himself. He made the congregation to which he was called to minister a
living band of Christ's Holy Catholic Church.
He did so both by precept and example.
Having acquired a large stock of knowledge
from the careful study of books, personal
observation and practical experience, he always
earnestly desired to impart the results at which
he had arrived. He did so forcibly, though
in the most impartial manner, acting upon the
conviction that men and women should think
for themselves, and form their own judgment.
This was a noticeable feature in all his sermons,
lectures and addresses. He most strongly
deprecated the idea that people should pin their
faith to any particular party, pet preacher or
favourite journal. He thought that Christians
should exercise their brains, as well as their
hearts and consciences. The sermons which he

preached on Sunday mornings invariably dealt
with matters of doctrine, or of exposition, and
were addressed particularly to the more cultured
members of the congregation. The sermons on
Sunday evenings were of a more practical type,
and generally directed to questions of conduct,
especially during the seasons of Advent and Lent.
Amongst the various courses may be mentioned—

> Some Common Faults.—Thoughtlessness, Evil-speaking,
> Conceit, Worldliness, Cant.
> Defects in Common Life.—Want of Sincerity, Want of
> Thoroughness, Want of Courtesy, Want of Progress,
> Want of Devotion.
> Some Faults of the Age —Impatience, Superficiality,
> Self-consciousness, False Pessimism, Sectarianism.
> The Christian in Common Life.—The Christian Gentle-
> man, The Christian Citizen, The Christian in Trade,
> The Christian in his Leisure, The Christian in his
> Home, The Christian Servant
> The Calls of Christ —The Call to Penitence, The Call
> to Holiness, The Call to Brotherhood, The Call to
> Service, The Call to Perseverance.
> Social Morality : the Last Six Commandments and Modern
> Life.—Society and the Individual, Parents and
> Children, Husband and Wife, Justice, Charity.
> The Making of Character.—Personality, Environment,
> Conscience, Choice, Habit, Perseverance.
> The Journey of Life.—Youth, Manhood, Middle Life,
> Old Age
> The Responsibility of Life.—The Purpose of Life, Life as
> a Race, Life as a Conflict, Life as a Work-Time,
> Life as an Education, The Life to Come.

" It was the custom to give each Registered
Member of St. Nicholas a card of Membership

at the Annual General Meeting of the congregation, on which a motto was inscribed for the year. In 1900, when the Rector was already sick unto death, he was asked to suggest the text as usual. He chose, ' Time is the stuff of which life is made '—' Be true to the end of the day, and the last load home.' And this may be said to have been the last message of Henry Cary Shuttleworth to the church which he served so faithfully, and to the people whom he loved so well."

One of Shuttleworth's colleagues at St. Nicholas Cole Abbey thus describes his methods in Divine Service—

" His great idea about Church worship, was to make it a delight. In his effort to do this he used every means he could command— flowers, lights, vestments, music, were with him a means to this end. I remember well one beautifully fine Whitsunday, when the sun was streaming into the church, finding him lighting up the candles of the big candelabrum in the middle of the church. I said to him, ' What on earth are you lighting those candles for, on a day like this ?' His reply was, ' My dear friend, looks pretty, looks pretty.' I think that with him the main delight was that of the artist, at the beauty of the symbol in itself, rather than of the philosopher in the adequate symbolical expression of an idea.

"But it was on music that he mainly relied to make Church worship a delight, and in this he succeeded up to the hilt. He took the greatest pains with his choir, which was a large and very excellent one, composed of men and women. Before I went to him, I had never heard what is called a High Celebration : and, averse as I always have felt to everything that might seem to make worship a thing distinct from conduct, I had expected not to like it. But I must confess that I was soon won over, and before long came to feel really helped and uplifted spiritually by beautiful music. On festivals, Gounod's 'Messe Solennelle' was always taken, and no words of mine can adequately describe the impression made on me on some sunshiny Easter Day with the church ablaze with flowers, a packed congregation, and this magnificent music, with organ and piano accompaniment, rolling round the little square building. The majestic words of the service, 'We praise Thee, we bless Thee, we worship Thee, we glorify Thee, we give thanks to Thee for Thy great glory, O Lord God, Heavenly King, God the Father Almighty,' seemed to mean more than ever before ; and, with the music, a great wave of indescribable emotion flashed through one's heart, leaving behind it a sense of having indeed been 'lifted up and strengthened.'

"Or on some Sunday afternoon, with, again, a packed church, to see the Rector standing just within the south-west corner of the rails, baton in hand, facing his choir, conducting Spohr's 'Calvary' or 'Last Judgment,' or Mendelssohn's 'Elijah' or 'Hymn of Praise,' was a sight not to be forgotten. His very frame seemed to expand under the excitement of the moment, and woe to those who, just before such a service, bothered him with commonplace remarks or questions. He was no dilettante conductor, gently displacing the air with timid beats (like a mother pretending to whip her spoilt child), and carefully following the time of the organist, his eyes never lifted from his score. As I have said, his very form seemed to dilate with enthusiam, his baton swept the air with the vigour of a Guardsman showing off his sword-practice, his left hand also (in particularly uplifting passages) being equally employed ; his face set aglow by the intensity of feeling as the music rolled around, and smote into sympathetic vibration every nerve of his system. He was indeed 'filled with the god,' and even a much less capable choir than was ours would, I believe, have responded to his leadership and—half hypnotized by his enthusiasm—would have taken difficult passages with a correctness and finish that would have astonished themselves.

"These afternoon 'Musics' were always crowded to excess. People used to come and wait outside the doors long before they were opened, and the regular congregation, not coming so early, often found themselves excluded. To prevent this, Shuttleworth invited the regular members to register themselves, and gave to each a card of Membership which admitted them to the church by a door which was opened a quarter of an hour before that by which the general public were admitted. This secured the desired result, and the regular church attenders got good seats."

Another clergyman who worked with Shuttleworth at St. Nicholas, has given this interesting account of his ideals and methods—

" I will not say much about my own relations with Henry Cary Shuttleworth at St. Nicholas Cole Abbey, lest I should become more autobiographical than biographical. I was then a comparatively old man: he a young one. When I first said the Litany there on the Feast

of the Conversion of St. Paul, 1884, and he
characteristically read a poem of Keble's
instead of preaching a sermon, I had passed
three septennial apprenticeships in the Church
and was older than he was at the end of his
noble fight in the Church Militant.   Though I
was the apprentice and he the master, he treated
me with an ever-kindly concern and patience,
and a tenderness like that of a strong son for a
father.   Indeed, I never had any other title
from him, in talk or in letters, but 'Father
Tom' or 'Dear Padre.'

"I felt at that glad time, as I had never before
done under any clerical leader, as if we were
going foward together, sure of triumph, into the
most hopeful of all battles, where the leader
had no fright lest the follower should contradict
his plans, or endanger his interests.   The pulpit of his parish was the first in which I felt
myself in possession of the most unfettered
liberty, where I need keep nothing back, where
I might speak out everything which I supposed
to be a part of the whole counsel of God.   The
eager spirit and much of the record of that
defiant early campaign may be found in the
volumes of the *Church Reformer*, which Mr.
Headlam kept up year after year at great cost
to himself.   The Rector, with rare courage, had

adopted it (in place of the innocuous pages of the magazine of the Young Men's Friendly Society) as the inside pages of his St. Nicholas Cole Abbey Magazine. The Rector's deliberate choice of such a paper, whether good or bad, was at least a very clear declaration where he meant to stand. Everything he did was chivalrous, and in the spirit of the consecrated knight who prefers the cause of the feeble and the wronged or the unrepresented to any other, because it must be the cause of God.

" The freedom which he gave to me he extended to all who preached in his pulpit. He wished to be as broad as he saw the Church to be ; hence no preacher ever need ask his licence to say, or his pardon for saying, things with which he himself did not agree. He was afraid lest Truth herself might be hurt by any attempts of his to gag men who said in sincerity what they thought to be true. He never failed in smart criticism afterwards.

" He succeeded in making St. Nicholas Cole Abbey—what every Cathedral and Parish Church in the land ought to be—a sight pleasant even in the eyes of such as do not ordinarily or ever go to church, except for Holy Matrimony or Holy Baptism, or at a funeral, and to whom the Separatist conscience therefore denies the right and liberty of entering their names in a census of religion. I remember one Sunday morning in that victorious time, when I could scarcely preach for the loud noise made by the bands of the serried multitudes of London wage-workers, who were marching through Queen Victoria Street with their banners from the East End and South of London to a demonstration in the West End. Some of their regiments burst forth into spontaneous cheering as they passed the Church of St. Nicholas Cole Abbey. Such a recognition of its clergyman, whom they knew to be so brotherly a man, occurred more than once.

"When Shuttleworth first began work at St. Nicholas Cole Abbey, he was keenly affected, like all his fellows in the Guild of St. Matthew, by the then victorious progress of the religious movement for ' Restoration' started by Mr. Henry George. Henry Shuttleworth always answered the call to share in any conflict against those wrongs which had been done for ages, and were still doing, against the poorest estate of wage-labourers. But he had learned from the young men and women whom he had gathered about him at St. Paul's

Cathedral, and from his large experiences as Organizing Secretary of the Young Men's Friendly Society, and it pressed on him more closely when he became so peculiarly the pastor of such young folk at St. Nicholas Cole Abbey, that modern society was providing a multitudinous estate of the neglected amongst the sons and daughters of the middle classes. The service of Mammon demands fresh blood, and pitilessly tramples down the old or middle-aged or useless. Lads and lasses are sent up in crowds out of the counties to London, that they may take the place once occupied by the sturdy 'London Apprentices' of English history, and serve in the shops and warehouses of Babylon to make the fortunes of their neighbours, though with no prospect, like the London apprentices of history, of making their own fortune, and with little security of a continuous earning of their own daily bread. It is due to the founders of the Young Men's Christian Association, and also to the memory of Dr. Binney, the Independent Minister (whose influence with young men in the City I well remember), to say that they attempted with all that was in them to find and to remedy the ill done by Babylon to its younger servants. But the Evangelical and Dissenting conception of

humane life was as contrary as possible to the
Catholic and Socialist conception of it.   It
assumed that a young man was not sent up to
London to serve the Church and Commonwealth of London, but to serve himself, to get
individual wealth; he was first to get good,
spiritual and material, and then to do good
with his goods, however gotten.   The ideal
New Man of the religious world was a new
Abraham; a Jacob, a Samuel Morley, a big
'Christian philanthropist,' one who was diligent
in the service of Mammon, with the honest
intention of becoming contemporaneously and
subsequently no less diligent in the service of
God, the common Father.   Particular Bibles
were composed for this peculiar religion.   The
most deeply studied of these were *The Successful Merchant*, the biography by a Wesleyan
Minister of an eminent disciple of this strange
Christian Mammonism, and the still more
famous *How to make the Best of Both Worlds*,
by Dr. Binney himself, the chief apostle of that
anti-social and anti-Christian faith.   It is a
satisfaction to know that Dr. Binney, who was
a really humane and social thinker at heart,
confessed in his latter days, when the Socialists
were exposing the misery of an eminent
hosier's workwomen, that he sincerely re-

pented of having written such a book. Dr.
Binney had been much impressed by the
renewal of life in the Church of London,
especially during the 'London Mission.' Still
more had his tone of thinking been revolution-
ized, like Baldwin Brown's and Dr. Dale's,
by the study of Maurice. Taking one of
the young members of his meeting into his
library at Walworth, and pointing to a row of
Maurice's books, he said to him, ' These are
my teachers.'

" Henry Shuttleworth, as Rector of the City
parishes united in St. Nicholas Cole Abbey,
was in many respects the City successor of this
Independent pastor of the King's Weigh-
House Chapel. I need hardly say that he was
enabled to become much more than Binney had
ever been, or could be, to the young men and
women pushed out of the counties into London,
not only by his inward character, education,
and gifts, but by his outward Catholic, national,
and parochial calling as an English priest.
The social and economical standing of the
classes for whose welfare Binney's generous
heart had been deeply stirred, presented itself
to Shuttleworth's Socialist mind in a very
different shape. He was quick to see that
their case was in many ways less hopeful than

was that of the mechanical wage-labourers, who were so richly provided with tribunes and spokesmen. The middle-class labourers in the shops and the warehouses of the City had only such insufficient champions as the good people who petitioned Mammon for early closing—which he was urgent also in demanding; or they had such inefficient friends as the preachers of the anti-apostolic doctrines, 'Touch not, taste not, handle not.' What he felt was how little share they had in the joy and freedom of life proper to the young, but so often out of reach when age has come. He saw that they were absolutely wanting in such social organizations as the trades-unions, and in such tribunes and leaders of their own estate, as gives to the artisan wage-labourer some degree of power to hold his own, for himself, for his family, and for his fellow-worker, against the tyranny and greed of the proud, the mighty and the rich.

" It was altogether in their interest that Henry Shuttleworth resolved that he would have some building besides the Parish Church. He knew well enough, as he frequently said, that in the Middle Ages, when the common thought of Christianity was in many respects broader, more humane, and more democratic than it now is, the naves of the Parish Church would have been employed without hesitation for all wholesome and neighbourly 'secular' purposes. But he was too good a ruler to disturb a prejudice unnecessarily, or where he knew that there was some good at the root of it. He began to be anxious about providing his numerous young folk with what he used first to call a 'Parish-House,'—a name not quite fit for it, as he needed it for the use of those who were properly members of other parishes. Many a parish, before the Puritan Abomination of Desolation swept over our land, was provided with a 'Church-House,' where the 'Church Ales' were brewed, where the neighbourly feasts were held, where dramas were performed by the parish play-actors. Of these common 'Church-Houses' some were expropriated by the Long Parliament; some of them were handed over to Puritan sectaries to serve as their meeting-houses, others were allowed to be seized by the local Puritan landlords and incorporated into their own estates.

" Henry Shuttleworth's constant thought and talk at that time was how he could collect funds to repair and furnish for such uses the old tower of the disestablished parish of St. Mary Somerset. The tower was and is still standing, though its nave has been pulled down, and its congregation united with that of St. Nicholas Cole Abbey, and its land, as I imagine, transferred from 'Sion to Babylon.' His scheme for the re-establishment and re-endowment of the tower of St. Mary Somerset, however, proved impracticable for reasons which I do not now recollect His plan finally took shape, as all the City of London knows, in his foundation of the St. Nicholas Club, to which he purposely gave an extra-parochial extension, and which the members fitly named the 'Shuttleworth Club.'

"Of this club I scarcely need speak; partly because nothing else that he did after he was made Rector of St. Nicholas added so much to his general popularity, nor was so widely appreciated, nor so fully described: partly also because there are so many, both of the clergy and laity, who are more familiar with it than ever I was, and therefore more competent than I am to speak in detail about it. Yet I give three facts concerning the origin of the 'Club' (manifesting his spirit in its erection and government), which I observed from the rudimentary beginning.

" First, ever since I knew him, he always had a sort of club of young folk about him, of which he was the President, though it was itinerant, and had no fixed home, until he became Rector of St. Nicholas.

"Next I observe that the Club, according to his idea and conduct of it, was meant to enjoy all possible freedom and self-government, and to serve as an instrument of neighbourly education. It was not to have the nature of a trap to 'attract' young men and women, and catch them for a Church-going to which they were ordinarily disinclined. It was not annexed to his Parish Church, nor to the English Church, although it was undoubtedly a product of that godly relation, which he knew the Church held towards all who are not in the Church, and which is expressed in our English phraseology of the union between Church and Common-wealth. His own attitude could not be better described than he himself has done by his description of Dr. Guy, his old schoolmaster, in the sermon which he preached at the funeral of that admirable educator. He assumed that all true-born Englishmen were elected and called to be Churchmen; and that all baptized Englishmen were fundamentally Catholics and Churchmen, whatever other kind of men they might fancy, fear, or boast themselves to be. This he had learned from Maurice, and for this

he contended at the Church Reform Union in his
discussions with Dr. Martineau upon 'Church
Reform,' and in what he wrote upon 'Home
Rule in the Church.'   It was a position which
Dr. Martineau, who ended at the point where
Maurice began, could not easily apprehend.
Dr. Martineau, in whom there was so much
more of the Nonconformist than of the
Separatist temper, never seemed quite able to
free his noble and profound spirit from the
tight traditional bonds of his early Unitarian
education.

" Lastly, as to the Club there can be no more
absurd mistake than the fancy that Henry
Shuttleworth first conceived of it as a place
wherein amusement, and junketings, carding,
dancing, and drinking, or other delights of
' Esau,' might be carried on more harmlessly
than they could outside it.   True it is that his
heart was always singularly tender towards
' Esau,' whose 'Chaplain' he had become by
the most free election, and not by the immoral-
ity of canvassing for Esau's vote.   He had a
fondness for Esau, while he had only tolerance
for ' Jacob,' whether Jacob wore Evangelical,
or Latitudinarian, or Catholic clothing.   He
was kindly towards Jacob, because his large
heart was kindly towards all, but it cannot be

said that he admired Jacob, or thought him exemplary, or that he enjoyed Jacob's society. One, who had applied to him as Priest, he sent to another Priest, saying, 'I am not a spiritual man.' It was an autobiographical slip, and, I think, more remarkable for its humility than its exactness. He was a born educator and director of the young. And it was as Esau's Chaplain, as he liked to be called, that he felt his own and Esau's want of the Club. 'Esau is a good fellow,' said he, 'but his prime want is education.'

" It was a constant sorrow to me that neither of the three Bishops of London under whom he served—Bishop Jackson, Bishop Temple, Bishop Creighton—ever secured him for the pastorate of some great and populous parish, wherein alone a full exercise, vent, and use might have been found for all his inward and outward gifts—his fascination over young and old, his talent for leadership, his bright common-sense, his adventuresomeness in fresh experiments, his powers of organization, the feeling of brotherly equality which he kindled in all, his gift for government, his facility in the conviction and conversion of gainsayers, his ever-acceptable fellowship with all sorts and conditions of men and women, his peculiar readiness

to eat and drink with publicans and sinners ;
his tolerance of spirit towards all that are without ; his English love of sport ; above all, his
apparently insatiable hunger for work.

"Moreover he was one of the few amongst our
contemporary priests who seemed quite clear in
the perception of what a Parish is according to
the belief and practice of the Church. He knew
that a Parish was the sole 'congregation'
recognized by the Church. He knew how it
differed from any aggregation gathered around
a preacher and parted by his own individual
effort ; he knew also how it differed from any
segregation gathered out of sundry parishes
upon the sectarian and sandy foundation of like-
mindedness in culture, in opinions and tastes.
He knew that the Parish was a congregation of
unlike-minded men which the Word of God
Himself had gathered into oneness and community by His ordering of history, and by His
rule over the personal and domestic life of each
man, woman and child. He knew that the Will
of God has congregated into each parish, as He
has done into each family and each national
Commonwealth, such diversities of persons as
would have dreamed of constituting themselves
into one body, and whose natural dream is that
they cannot properly be what He has made

K

them, in spite of their own wills and their own
opinions, to be, really the members one of
another in the same body. It is not in a self-
imagined inward unity of the like-minded and
like-conditioned (which is the creation of our
own wills and tastes), but it is in the *outward
conformity of the unlike-minded* and unlike-con-
ditioned (which is the social creation of the
common Father) that we discern the valid
mark of the Catholic Church. Many a long
talk he and I had together over this matter,
especially during the early years of his
ministry at St. Nicholas Cole Abbey. I always
came away from his study, that ever-fresh centre
of spiritual light and heat in the dark City of
London, feeling what a waste of God's rich gifts
was being made by a careless Church, and what
thousands of souls might have been saved,
illuminated, refreshed and elevated if one of
the great London parishes had been put by
authority under his care."

The "Shuttleworth Club," with all that it
implied and involved, formed so important an
element in the later life of its founder, that
some further particulars of its origin and growth
are essential to a true understanding of his
history and work.

It would be difficult to fix upon the time

when the idea of establishing a club for the benefit of the men and women of the City of London first entered Shuttleworth's mind. From the early days of his curacy at Oxford the pressing need of social organizations for rational recreation and amusement in connexion with the activities of Church and Parish had impressed him ; and the various clubs and guilds which he started at St. Barnabas, and the personal interest which he took in the boys and young men of the town, showed that he had thus early in his career a definite conception of the place which amusement should take in social and parochial life.

Later on, during his term of office at St. Paul's Cathedral, the needs of the young men employed in the warehouses of the City became known to him, and he was one of the active promoters of the St. Paul's Cathedral Club, which was successfully carried on for several years.

In January 1884 Shuttleworth entered upon his new work as Rector of St. Nicholas Cole Abbey. The story of his first coming to the church has been told already, and the magical change which was effected in a few weeks surprised all who knew what City churches were wont to be. Where a mere handful of

people had leisurely come together, overflowing
congregations gathered round the doors await-
ing the opening of the church. The regular
worshippers at St. Nicholas even in those early
days were not parishioners, or residents of the
City, but people, mostly young men and women,
whose occupations brought them into the
neighbourhood of the church on week-days,
and who, at some time, either at St. Paul's or
in some other way, had been brought under
the magnetic influence of the new Rector.
Congregation, choir, and officials came from
various districts of London, many of them from
outlying suburbs, and it was difficult for the
Rector to get to know his people, or for the
people to become known to each other.

From the beginning, the Rector found his
work hindered and his many plans for in-
creasing the usefulness of the church made
hard of achievement by the want of a place in
which his large and scattered congregation
could meet. In his second Pastoral Address,
issued in January 1885, after the completion of
his first year's work, he said : " The more I
come to see the needs of our work at St.
Nicholas, the more clearly it grows upon me
that we want a Parish-House or Club, with
Lecture-Room and Drawing-Room. The great

expense of a house in the City will make this very hard of attainment. Still the need will be seen some day by others besides ourselves, and then we may be helped to supply it. At present we have no place but the church in which we can meet, or talk, or learn together." In the spring of 1885 the new Rectory-House of St. Nicholas on Lambeth Hill was completed, and it became the centre for such meetings and re-unions as could be accommodated. With lavish hospitality the Rector threw open his house to his people, and from early morning to late at night he was ready on all occasions to welcome any one and every one who had need of help, rest, or refreshment. But space at the Rectory was necessarily limited, and the problem of a meeting-place for his people was ever before the Rector. It occurred to him to try and utilize the old tower of St. Mary Somerset in Thames Street, which had been left standing after the destruction of the church and the amalgamation of the parish with that of St. Nicholas. In February 1885 the Rector wrote—

" The City Lands Committee have kindly allowed me, at a nominal rent, to become tenant of the disused tower of St. Mary Somerset, which stands in Thames Street, at the corner of Lambeth Hill, close to the new parsonage-house. When the church was pulled down the tower was preserved, not so much for its beauty as for its interest. It has never been occupied, except by pigeons, and some money must be spent on the interior if I am to make it of use, as I hope to do, for parish purposes. I don't know where this money is to come from, but I must try my hand at begging! What a pity there is not space in the tower for our much-needed lecture-hall and other rooms! Who will find us a room or the rent for a house not too far from the church ? "

In July of the same year he said · " We must raise about £300 for the fitting up of the tower of St. Mary Somerset. My great dream is to take a good house and make it into a Parish Club, with class-rooms, reading, and recreation-rooms. With this an idea strongly upheld by Mr. Hancock might some day be combined. It is not directly connected with the parish, but I should like to take a few young men studying for Holy Orders and see if a modest Clergy-School, with opportunities for working in London, could not be carried out. But the Parish-House, to say nothing of this, is far away in the clouds at present. The tower of St. Mary Somerset will serve as a very fair pilot-balloon to show us if the larger scheme of a

Parish-House would really be likely to succeed. I propose to fit up three or four rooms in the tower, and to use them for class-rooms of various kinds. One room will have newspapers and magazines, and possibly tea and coffee may be supplied."

It was to assist in raising the funds for fitting up the Tower that the Rector published a little volume of songs and verses which made its appearance in October 1885, and was announced by its author as follows: "I have done it! I knew I should! I have printed a little book of verses, and I am going to print some of the lectures I have given at St. Nicholas. I have often thought that among all melancholy monuments of human folly, the most utterly depressing are the publication of tenth-rate verses and commonplace sermons. I am sorely oppressed by the consciousness that I am adding a specimen of either kind to a museum of vanities already sufficiently appalling. My only consolation is, that as the verses are to be sold for the Restoration Fund of St. Mary Somerset Tower, the deed has been done in the hope of turning an honest penny in a good cause." Various entertainments were organized from time to time to get money for the Fund, but the project did not commend itself very strongly to the congregation of the church, and effort soon flagged.

With the introduction of the Lectures and Oratorios on Sunday afternoons, the difficulties of the situation increased. Afternoon Teas at the Rectory became an institution for those who lived at a distance and would have been unable to return for the Evening Service, and so many availed themselves of the standing invitation that the resources of the Rectory were severely taxed. As time went on the need for accommodation for parish purposes increased, and the idea of the Club-House was ever in the Rector's mind, and his hopes and wishes in regard to it ever on his tongue. Again and again he is found referring to his dream: "We want a Parish-House or Club; we want Class-Rooms; and we should like a large Lecture-Room or Hall. In one word, we want money." Writing at Christmas-time in 1888 he said—

"Good fairies who come down with purses of gold are not too plentiful outside the Christmas magazines, and the pantomimes or melodramas. But if any such good fairy should chance to read these lines, let me point out that we are greatly in need of money here at St. Nicholas, wherewith to carry on manifold works acknowledged to be good; and, in particular, that we are starved, cramped, paralyzed, for want of room in which to grow.   For want of *a* room, perhaps I should have said : we have no schools available, no vestry of a useful size, no room of any sort except the church and the Rectory.   The rents here in the City are so enormous that, if we could find a room or rooms large enough and suitable for our purposes, it would cost us at least £200 a year for our rent.   What couldn't we do if we had that ? what dreams would we not endeavour to realize ? what plans might we not carry out ?   I fairly get disheartened over it, when I think of it ; for I see no way out of it, unless through the appearance, out of the blue, of the good fairy.   And good fairies of that sort are scarce.   I found myself, on Christmas Day itself, waking from a day-dream of a well-appointed Parish-Hall, to rage at the impotence of my own poverty."

In his Pastoral Address, dated January 1889, the Rector announced his intention of abandoning the idea of making use of the Tower—"I have resolved to suspend, for the present, the endeavour to restore the tower of St. Mary Somerset.   I find that the cost would be far heavier than I thought, while the space available would be very small, and not particularly convenient.   The same sum would secure us the rent of a commodious Parish-Room for two or three years, and I think that would be better worth our while." In March of the same year the great dream began to seem as if it might some time be realized, for he then wrote—

"I think that the time has come when we must get Parish-Rooms somehow, or the whole of our work will starve. I have long felt that this was our great need, and it has now become so pressing that unless it can be met we shall be paralyzed I have my eye on two floors which would suit us excellently well in many respects ; but the rent is £250! We are hardly likely, I fear, to get anything suitable for much less than that ; and I shall not commit myself to so great a responsibility until I can see my way clear to the rent for three years at least, and to the cost of furnishing simply. A generous friend has offered £100 a year for three years, provided the rooms are opened, at latest, by September ; and another has offered a handsome contribution to the furniture. Upon this my present idea is to make an appeal to my own friends, and to all who are interested in our work here, to guarantee the rest of the rent for three years. After that— but sufficient unto the day ! For the working expenses I think we can trust to the place itself, if it is large enough, as it needs must be, to hold our entertainments and social gatherings in. A Library and Reading-Room, with a Lecture-Room, would, of course, be part of the institution ; and I particularly want a Drawing-Room for the ladies, to which they might ask their friends — occasionally even their male friends."

In April he said: "The die is cast! I have not actually signed the agreement, but I have practically taken the two floors at 81A, Queen Victoria Street, for Parish-Rooms, and I am responsible for the rent. Now comes the rub. I must get the rent somehow, and, as soon as the close of Term at King's College sets me comparatively free, I shall begin to worry friends and neighbours all round. I don't mean to appeal to the congregation in general. I think the rent ought to come from outside, and then we can manage the working expenses ourselves. But if any of you know of any friend who is well disposed to the sort of work we do here, and would be willing to help us, pray tell such a one that I want £1000 for these rooms to form a social centre for our people, and to develop classes and lectures and organizations in connexion therewith. I shall be glad of a lump sum down, or of subscriptions spread over three years. I need not point out once again how our work here has been crippled and starved for want of any room but the Church and Rectory, and how under the peculiar

conditions of our congregation we especially
need Parish-Rooms. The venture I have made
is not a light one, and I feel the responsibility
of having to raise so large a sum, and probably
to do it again in three years' time. But I am
sure that it has got to be done, if the work
begun here is to be maintained and developed;
and I must trust to the kindness of friends and
sympathizers to see me through it."

A circular was subsequently issued in the
following terms : " The Church of St. Nicholas
Cole Abbey is attended by large numbers of
young men employed in the warehouses and
other places of business in the City. The
work done among them by the Rector of St.
Nicholas (Rev. H. C. Shuttleworth) during
the last twelve years has been widely
appreciated, and has attracted considerable
notice.

" Mr. Shuttleworth feels that his work has
now reached a point when it must languish and
starve unless he can provide rooms for classes,
lectures, meetings, and social gatherings, so as
to form a centre for the various organizations
of a well-worked church. In an ordinary parish
this would be comparatively easy; but in the
case of St. Nicholas there is no available room
of any kind, and the resources of the Rectory

have been severely taxed in an endeavour to meet the growing need.

"By the kindness of a few friends, Mr. Shuttleworth has got together a sum of over £700. He has therefore taken two floors of a warehouse at 81A, Queen Victoria Street, close to the church; and he now appeals to his parishioners and friends and to those who know something of what he has done for the young people of the City, for a further sum of £500. This amount will be devoted to the heavy expense of fitting up and furnishing the rooms, and especially to meeting the rent, £250 per annum, for the next three years or more. The Rector guarantees to make the rooms pay their own working expenses, if the rent and the first cost can be found from outside.

" It is intended that the rooms shall include, (*a*) a Lecture-Room and Class-Room; (*b*) a Library; (*c*) a Smoking-Room for men ; (*d*) a large room available for concerts or social gatherings, which, when not so employed, will be a Drawing-Room for women, with books, papers, chess, etc. It is proposed that gentlemen may be invited to the Drawing-Room during certain defined hours, when the Rector and Mrs. Shuttleworth will be present, or some other lady and gentleman on their behalf.

" Arrangements will be made for supplying light refreshments, tea, coffee, etc.

" It is hoped that the rooms will thus provide the advantages of a Club, with opportunities for culture, amusement, and for that healthy social intercourse in which the ordinary life of young men and women engaged in the City is sadly lacking.

" No religious test will be imposed upon those using the rooms ; but the work will be carried on in a reasonable religious spirit, in connexion with the church of St. Nicholas."

In his monthly notes in the Parish Magazine of July 1889 the Rector further expressed his view with regard to the club that was to be : " The Parish-Rooms are situated at the end of a long passage, and up a staircase, at 81A, Queen Victoria Street, nearly opposite the church. The windows look into the Rectory garden. The landlords have made the slight alterations which they undertook to do, and our friend Mr. Aldam Heaton is now setting his carpenters and decorators to work at partitions, and other necessary changes in the aspect and appearance of the place. It will be opened, I hope, in September, probably in connexion with the Dedication Festival, which we usually keep at the end of that month. My idea at present is that the rooms shall be open to all Registered Members, on payment of an annual subscription, the amount of which will be fixed as low as possible. Friends and out- siders may be introduced under conditions which have yet to be framed. There will be frequent lectures, entertainments, classes, and so forth. The rooms will of course be open on Sundays. The first floor will be fitted up as a drawing-room for ladies, with books, papers, games, etc. At one end there will be a dressing-room and lavatory, and in front of this a permanent platform or stage to be used when entertainments or meetings are held in this room. The upper floor will be partitioned into three divisions—a smoking-room for gentle- men, with a lavatory ; a refreshment-room, and a small class-room, which can be also used as a writing-room, or a retreat for the ladies when their drawing-room is required for a lecture or entertainment. The refreshment-room can at any time be thrown into the smoking-room by the removal of the partition, so as to give space for smoking-concerts or other gatherings. We shall have to put up with some small incon- veniences, owing to the lack of space, unless we are enabled to take more rooms. I look for- ward to the opening of these rooms as by far

the most important event of my incumbency
here; and those who have so generously
helped me with funds will always have my
warmest gratitude, and yours also. It will be
seen that the Club will be open alike to ladies
and gentlemen. This experiment may perhaps
be regarded in some quarters as rather a risky
one. I don't believe that there is any serious
risk about it. Why should not our young
people meet together? and where can they
meet at present, except in the street? I
believe that the provision of means of healthy
social intercourse, like this Club of ours, is
about the best thing that can be done for the
young men and women who earn their living
in the City. At any rate, we shall see. The
Charity Commissioners are giving grants of
many thousand pounds to institutions in all
parts of London, and the money will come
from the funds of City charities. It will
scarcely be fair to pass by the City altogether.
For example, they will undoubtedly take a
considerable annual income from one of the
parishes of which I am Rector. Yet I am
obliged to take a responsibility of £250 a year
and more, upon myself, and beg right and left,
in order to meet the needs of the very district
for whose services these large sums were

originally left! The Commissioners seem to some extent to share the common delusion that there is 'nobody in the City.'"

The Club was used for the first time on Sunday, 22nd September, 1889, before the alterations were entirely finished; but in the course of a few weeks things were in good order. The Rector, with his overflowing generosity, stripped his own study of book-shelves, and comfortable chairs and sofas, to adorn the Clubrooms, and no one who joined the St. Nicholas circle in those early days can ever forget the delight and satisfaction which the Rector found in this realization of a long-cherished dream; the plans he formed, the air-castles he built, and the schemes he evolved for the enjoyment of his "boys and girls," made those early days of the Club one of the happiest of memories. In October 1889 he wrote—

" The great event of the hour is the opening of the St. Nicholas Club and Parish-Rooms at 81A, Queen Victoria Street. They are later in the field than I had hoped; and we shall hardly get into regular working order at once. Things must grow. Still, it is a great matter to have got the rooms at all; indeed, I look upon them as the most important event of my work here."

L

At the same time a circular was issued as follows—

ST. NICHOLAS CLUB,

81A, QUEEN VICTORIA STREET.

Annual Subscription, half-a-guinea. Entrance fee, three shillings and sixpence.

A few original Members can still join without entrance fee. Application to be made to the Rector.

Drawing-room for Ladies, Smoking-room, Refreshment-room, etc. The Library is not yet in order.

On the first Monday in each month an entertainment will be given at the Club. The Inaugural Entertainment will take place on the 7th October at 8 p m., under the direction of Mr. Alfred Capper, who will be assisted by Mr. Charles Capper, Mr. Fred Cape, and others. Admission, one shilling. Members of the Club, sixpence. Season Tickets, admitting to all the Club entertainments for the season, five shillings. Members, half-a-crown. Six entertainments will be given for this ticket.

The Rector will give a course of Lectures on "English Poets and Poetry of to-day," on the third Monday of each month, at 8 p.m., as follows—

October 21st	.	.	TENNYSON.
November 18th.	.	.	ROBERT BROWNING.
December 16th.	.	.	MATTHEW ARNOLD.
January 20th	.	.	ALGERNON CHARLES SWINBURNE.
February 17th	.	.	WILLIAM MORRIS, etc.
March 17th	.	.	MINOR POETS.

This course may possibly be continued in April and May. Fee for the course, half-a-crown. Club Members, one shilling. Single Lecture, sixpence. Club Members, threepence.

Miscellaneous Lectures will be given on the last Wednesday in each month, or by announcement. The first will be on 30th October, " The City of London, as it was, and as it is," by Mr. G. H. Birch, F.S.A. Admission, sixpence. Club Members, free.

The proceeds of all these Lectures and Entertainments will be given to the Club Funds.

Refreshments can be had at the Club, and it is hoped that in the future this department may be considerably developed.

When the first hundred, or original Members, have all sent in their names, they will be called together at a business meeting, for the purpose of drawing up rules, and deciding upon future action."

The Club at this time was open daily from 4 to 11 p.m., on Saturdays from 1 to 11, and on Sundays from 12.15 to 10.

Writing at the end of November 1889 the Rector said—

"The St. Nicholas Club may be unhesitat-
ingly described as a big success. The rooms
are thoroughly well used, the number of members increases rapidly, and all seems to be going
as well as possible. The place appears to be
what I hoped it would become—a social centre
for our people, where they can meet their
friends, enjoy a quiet hour's rest, or reading,
or conversation, or spend a pleasant and soci-
able evening. The lectures and entertainments
have been well attended, and though the prices
are very low, there has been a steady profit,
which goes to the 'rent and furnishing' fund.
The library is now being arranged and organized ; and when the billiard-table arrives, we
shall hope to go ahead yet more quickly.

"Mr. Clement O. Skilbeck, son of our much-
esteemed churchwarden of St. Mary Somerset,
has painted a very charming sign which hangs
over the Club doors. Saint Nicholas, in his
monastic robe and girdle, holding the Eastern
form of pastoral staff, stands beneath a tree
bearing his traditional three golden apples.
No hollow-cheeked and blear-eyed patron he,
but ruddy, wide-browed, firm-lipped man, with
human sympathies, keen insight, and quick
sense of humour marked upon the face. This
is a saint of the human sort, not of the diseased
ascetic type. One can fancy this St. Nicholas
setting booby-traps for his monks on the top
of their cell doors, as it was said St. Philip
Neri, founder of the Oratorians, used to do. The

noble motto around the figure exactly expresses the object with which the St. Nicholas Club was conceived and set on foot. ' Fellowship is Heaven, and the lack of fellowship is hell.' The words are those of John Ball, the famous ' mad priest ' of Kent, as the landlords of his time called him. This generation has begun to see that he was a prophet as well as a priest; one of the men born before their time, whose ideas and thoughts are not accepted by the world until they themselves have long lain in the grave, and are then hailed as a new Gospel. John Ball died four centuries ago ; and we think Christian Socialism is something strange and new ! "

In his Pastoral Address, dated 2nd February, 1890, the Rector said · " The great event of the year, I need not say, has been the opening of the St. Nicholas Club ; in which I have seen the fulfilment of my dream of many years. Certainly, up to the present time, the Club is a success more brilliant than my wildest fancy ventured upon. As a means of healthy recreation, and social intercourse, it could scarcely fulfil its purpose better than it does. We shall do a public service if we can show that a club composed of men and women can in all respects succeed. It is, indeed, a heavy responsibility for me ; not at present in the

sense of administration or government, for most
efficient and willing officers and helpers bear
the weight of the work ; and so far our sky has
been without serious cloud.   But the financial
burden is no light one ; and I am anxious now
to multiply the number of Honorary Members,
that we may have a certain yearly income to
depend upon for the heavy rent."

The first General Meeting of the Club took
place on 11th November, 1890, when a resolution was passed to increase the annual subscription to one guinea,[1] with an entrance fee of
five shillings ; and it was also decided to issue
an appeal to members to obtain contributions
towards the rent of the Club premises, over and
above the ordinary subscription.

The following are some extracts from the
first report of the Club's progress—

"Your Committee, in presenting the first
report of the St. Nicholas Club, is of opinion
that its members and friends are to be warmly
congratulated upon the success of a bold
venture.   That such a club was needed in the
City, our first year of life has abundantly
proved, and we cannot refrain from expressing
some surprise that the initiative was taken by

[1] Reduced to its former amount of half-a-guinea in the
following year.

no public body, but by a private individual, with the help and counsel of his own friends. The St. Nicholas Club is not absolutely the first which has been established in the City. Our President had previously been concerned in the foundation of the St. Paul's Cathedral Club; and there are others of a similar sort connected with the Y.M.C.A., the C.E.Y.M.S., etc. But this is the first club of its kind, and one of the few clubs in London which has ventured to admit both men and women as members. There were those who prophesied disaster as the result of this new departure; but the question had been carefully considered before the step was taken, and your Committee are of opinion that, so far as the first year can be regarded as a trial, the experiment has proved completely successful. They would venture to add that the responsibility of justifying it in the future rests with the members themselves. The St. Nicholas Club will have accomplished a wider and more beneficial success than that of finding a pleasant home for its members, it will have rendered a solid public service, if it should prove to the world that both sexes can meet as fellow-members of an institution like this, upon entirely equal terms, to their great mutual advantage.

"We have now, in round numbers, two hundred and eighty members upon the books, of whom one hundred and ten are women.

"Of the various activities which may be looked upon as in some sense branches of the Club, we may mention first, the lectures upon 'English Poets and Poetry,' given by the Rector during last winter. These attracted large audiences, and though the fee was merely nominal, they realized a good profit for the Club. The entertainments have consisted chiefly of concerts, given monthly during the winter. These also have brought in a substantial sum, besides furnishing entertainments of a high order.

"The lectures and entertainments are discontinued in the summer, and the energies of the members are directed to the cricket and tennis grounds we rent at Bowes Park. Both the cricket and tennis clubs, the latter especially, have had a successful season; and the boating members of the St. Nicholas Club have associated themselves with the Falcon Rowing Club, of which our President has for some years been an Honorary Member. A Cycling Club is also projected, and the President hopes to be able to provide a place for keeping machines belonging to members in the tower of

St. Mary Somerset, which he rents under the City of London.

"Monthly Cinderella dances are organized during the winter months, for members and their friends, at Anderton's Hotel. These have been in every way successful.

"The more serious side of life has not been neglected. The library is the centre of various endeavours to provide means for mutual culture and intellectual development. A Field Club has made scientific excursions into the country on Saturday afternoons, and the members propose studying geology together during the coming winter, visiting the Jermyn Street Museum, meeting at the Club for reading and conversation on the subject. A microscope, and small but excellent telescope, are available for any who are competent to use them. Meetings for informal conversation upon stated subjects have been held at frequent intervals, and have been found at once useful and interesting by those who have attended. Members with archæological proclivities have taken part in the proceedings of the East London Antiquarian Society.

"A few of our members, with our Vice-President, Mr. Allen, for their chief, organized and carried out a joint holiday upon the coast of South Wales; taking a house, and securing an inexpensive and delightful summer outing. It seems to your Committee that this plan is capable of being carried out upon a larger scale; and for next year a Swiss tour is proposed.

"The debates held monthly under the auspices of the Guild of St. Mary and St. Nicholas, and the good work done by the Ladies' Working Society, are not strictly branches of the Club. These two Societies hold their meetings in the Club drawing-room, giving a yearly contribution to the Club funds.

"One point alone remains for your Committee to notice. When the Club was established, the Rector made himself personally responsible for the heavy annual rent of £250, and he also collected a large sum from friends for the fitting up and furnishing of the premises.

"Your Committee is of opinion that the time has now come for an effort on the part of the members themselves, for whom the Club provides so many comforts, to share this burden with their President and Founder; and, in concluding this report, desires to make an earnest appeal to all members who can give a yearly contribution towards the rent, however small, to do so; or to bring the Club and its needs before the notice of such friends as may be able and willing to subscribe towards the rent, or to assist in getting rid of the debt which, as will be seen, still remains upon the cost of furnishing and fitting up the rooms."

After the General Meeting, the President issued the following letter, which was sent to all members of the Club—

" This letter is sent to you in consequence of the following resolution carried at the recent Annual General Meeting of Members of the Club—

> ' That an appeal be now made to every member of the Club to give or get, according to ability, a stated contribution towards the rent of the Club premises, over and above the ordinary subscription. Such contribution to be paid monthly, quarterly, or yearly, to the Rector, or his deputy, and acknowledged by him ; the several sums guaranteed not to be made public.'

" You are probably aware that I am at present personally responsible for the annual rent of the Club premises (£250). I do not wish to escape from a responsibility which I assumed deliberately ; although I confess that I should be very grateful if it were lightened in the way now

proposed. But I feel very strongly that the
Club ought not to depend upon my personal
exertions in getting money. Not only is our
independence thus taken from us, but the whole
position of the Club is rendered uncertain and
unstable. If I were to die, or to be sent to
some other parish, the Club would have to
find its own rent somehow, or dissolve. I am
very anxious that it should now be placed upon
a secure and permanent basis by the voluntary
efforts of its own members. We have now
two hundred and eighty upon the books; so
that if each could guarantee to give or get
£1 a year, the rent would be more than
cleared. I know that this is more than some
of us could undertake; but some, on the other
hand, may be able to do more. At any rate,
for the Club's sake rather than my own, I ask
you to do what you can, and to return the
accompanying form, duly filled up, at your
earliest convenience."

In the Rector's Pastoral Address written in
February 1891, he says of the Club: "It has
achieved a remarkable success, and it has done
great things for us, in many directions. Perhaps
the most solid service it has rendered us as a
congregation is this: it has made us into a real
society. Before the Club was, we scarcely

knew one another, though we worshipped here together.   Now, we meet so constantly that friendship is no longer an impossibility.   The Club has done for us what the bond of neighbourhood does for those who not only worship together but live side by side.   That is a great gain ; not the least of the many which have come to us through the Club."

The Rector's notes in the Parish Magazine for July 1891 contain a paragraph concerning some old houses which then stood at the end of the Rectory garden, and as these were occupying the site of the future Shuttleworth Club, the reference may be of interest—

" The old houses in Fye Foot Lane, at the end of the Rectory garden, have changed owners, and are likely, I understand, to be pulled down.   This will be a very great nuisance and inconvenience to me personally, and to the Club also ; for it will scarcely be possible to open any windows during the process of destruction.   As for my poor little garden, I suppose it will be trampled to pieces ; and the creepers, which it has taken some years to grow and train, can scarcely survive the removal of the walls against which they climb.   The houses themselves are in a very bad state, and ought to come down without question.   But that does not make it less inconvenient to us. When the rebuilding comes to the front, I shall have something to say in regard to the matter of light."

In the month of November 1891 the experiment of providing midday dinners and hot luncheons was made; and from this time the Club opened daily at 12.30 p.m. instead of 4 p.m.

In the spring of 1892 the St. Paul's Cathedral Club was dissolved; and many of its members joined the St. Nicholas Club under special arrangements. Most of the furniture, books, and other effects of the Club were purchased on behalf of the St. Nicholas Club, and the influx of new members made it necessary to extend the premises by the addition of another room. In August 1892 the Rector wrote—

"The opening of the new billiard-room at the Club will so greatly increase our accommodation that I hope to develop the educational side of our work more satisfactorily in the coming winter. I shall be glad if it prove practicable to set on foot some classes or circles for definite study. The new room will add over £100 to our present rent of £250; and there are of course expenses of adaptation and fitting up. These last, however, I see my way to meet out of special donations ; that is, unless they considerably exceed my estimate. The additional rent, however, is a serious and permanent responsibility ; and I shall be sincerely glad of any assistance which those who have not yet supported the Rent and Maintenance Fund may be in a position to offer."

In November 1892 the first idea of acquiring the present site seems to have occurred to the Rector, although at that time he seems to have had other plans with regard to it, for he writes—

" I have now the offer of a piece of land close to the Club, on very advantageous terms ; and I could build my much-desired boarding-house for women employed in the City, if I knew where to find some £3000. But I don't ; and I suppose the chance will slip through my fingers, never to come back. I hesitate to enter upon this or upon any other scheme of the many I have in mind, so long as the debt upon the Club remains so heavy."

In October, at the Annual General Meeting of the Club, it was resolved to increase the subscription to fifteen shillings a year, and writing at this time the Rector says—

"The main interest of St. Nicholas has of late gathered round the Club. The problem of raising funds to meet the heavy annual rent, and to pay off the present debt of £200, has become seriously pressing; and at the General Meeting a very strong feeling was expressed that something must be done. Many of the new members took up the matter with much warmth; and a second General Meeting was called to discuss possibilities. By resolution the subscription is to be fifteen shillings after this year for all town members, unless they represent to the President that they really are unable to pay more than the present half-guinea, and in these cases the excess may be remitted. A subsequent resolution for the reorganization of the Rent and Maintenance Fund was also carried, as a necessary supplement to the alteration of subscription."

From the time that the old houses in Fye Foot Lane were condemned, the Rector's one idea and longing was to be able to acquire the land upon which they stood, as he was aware that certain rights which he held in regard to "Ancient Lights" would give him great advantages in negotiating its purchase. The public announcement of his design to build a new Club-House was made in the autumn of 1893, at the Annual General Meeting of the Club, and in April 1894 we find him writing—

"The plans of the proposed new club premises make my mouth water. With such a Club-House, what could we not do, freed from the crushing burden of our present rent! The money comes in very slowly. To some hundred of written letters, addressed to City firms, I have received just *four* answers, two of them enclosing donations amounting to four guineas, the other two politely declining on account of heavy local claims. On the other hand, I have myself made or shall have made when my current courses of lectures are finished, something like £350 towards the Building Fund, in less than five months, besides a few very kind contributions from friends who have attended the lectures. It looks as if the wealthy City of London were going to leave the social well-being of its *employés* to the care of a penniless parson! One firm, however, that of Messrs. J. & R. Morley has, as always, helped us generously. I mean to get that £5000 somehow, whether the City helps or holds aloof. The only question is whether we shall have our Club with its own premises built on its own freehold, a permanent possession for the workers of the City; or whether we shall have it saddled with a ground-rent and a debt to hamper and hinder the institution in all its future undertakings. A little generous and timely help *now* would mean twice as much to us as it would mean hereafter. Among other things, it would mean

M

that my hair would still be black when the new Club is opened, instead of prematurely grey ; a trifling consideration, perhaps, but yet not without interest to me and mine "

Two months later (June 1894) he wrote—

" The new Club premises will be begun, I hope, almost immediately. A friend has offered to buy the site from me on very favourable terms, and to give me the right of repurchase for seven years. This has the advantage of giving me enough money in hand to commence building, and of extending the time during which I can get the purchase-money together. So that, before very long—as soon indeed as the legal business can be got through—the old cottages will come down, and the new walls will begin to rise."

Writing late in October of the same year, he said—

" I should like, if it were possible, to enter our new Club premises next Lady Day free from debt ; but that involves the collection of £2275 for the building, to which another £500 must be added for fittings and furniture. Of this I have only about £400 in hand ; and a promise of £500 more, if the balance is collected by the end of this year. I should have thought that there were four people in the City of London who could and would each meet the promised £500 with a like sum. If only I could find those four, I could go steadily to work and get back the freehold within the seven years of grace."

An endeavour was made by the members of the Club to raise one sum of £500, but only £400 was collected. In December 1894 the Rector, writing of the progress of affairs, said—

"The holders of collecting-cards for the Club Building Fund have not only worked hard, but with considerable success. The sum which has at present come to hand is, however, below the £500 which is required; and the efforts of our energetic fellow-workers will need to be continued, even redoubled, if we are to claim our friend's promise before the few remaining days of grace expire. Meanwhile the builders have not been idle, and the brickwork is finished and the roof on, before the frosts come. Much of the interior woodwork is also completed, and only needs bringing to the place and fixing in position; then will follow the plastering, fitting up, and the final stages of preparation for the opening by the Lord Mayor. The matter of payment for our pretty and convenient new home is now the pressing matter."

In February 1895 a Special Meeting was held at the old Club to consider the question of raising the subscription in view of the change to the new premises, and it was eventually decided that the subscription should be raised from fifteen shillings to a guinea for men, the women to pay fifteen shillings as before. At this meeting it was proposed that the name of the Club should be changed, and that, on taking possession of its new house, it should be known as the " Shuttleworth Club" instead of " St. Nicholas Club." The Rector being unable to be present at this meeting, subsequently wrote as follows—

" Some conversation took place at the General Meeting of the Club last month in regard to an alteration in the title of the institution. I shall be sorry, for many reasons, to part with the name of ' St. Nicholas,' if it should seem necessary to change it. But I have reason to believe that in spite of all our efforts to prevent it, the present name leads to misunderstanding as to the scope and basis of the Club ; people who know little about it not unnaturally take it for granted that it is limited to the parish, or to connexion with St. Nicholas Church, and we lose members. I have enquired into the facts, and I am assured that this is undeniable. Moreover, we have to consider the future. I may possibly have successors in the Rectory who would very reasonably object to a club at the very gates, bearing the name of ' St.

Nicholas,' while unattached to the church or the parish, and with which the Rector might prefer to have nothing to do. This might become a very serious difficulty; and if we change at all, our entry into new quarters is manifestly the best time for the alteration. As to our new title, I was approached some time ago with a request that it might be called by my own name. I felt this to be a great honour to myself; and I should suppose that no man could be other than gratified at the prospect of thus keeping his memory green in the place where he had lived and worked; and that place the City of London. The only objection I could feel is this; that it looks a little like the self-advertisement which I loathe, I think, more than I can find words adequately to express. But if it is really the wish of my friends and fellow-members to do me and mine this graceful courtesy, I could not refuse it. I should accept it less as a tribute to myself, than to the principles and ideas upon which the club is founded, and in the pursuit of which I hope and pray that, under whatever title, it long may flourish and increase."

The opening of the new Club-House took place on the 12th June, 1895, the ceremony being performed by the Lord Mayor; and the Sixth Annual Report of the Club read at the meeting of members on 25th November, 1895, shows the position of affairs at this time—

"*New Buildings and New Name.*—The opportunity afforded by the change of quarters has been used for the purpose of changing the title by which the Club has hitherto been known. There are not a few who regret the loss of the name of 'St. Nicholas Club' which had become invested with so many pleasant associations, but experience proved that it was impossible to get rid of the impression that a Club so titled was in some way a Church Society or parochial organization, instead of being, as is and always has been the fact, freely open to all without question of religious beliefs, and only connected with the parish of St. Nicholas by locality, and by the circumstance that it was founded by the Rector. A change of name being found necessary it was decided by the members at a Special General Meeting, that the Club should henceforward bear the name of its founder, and be known as the Shuttleworth Club.

" The new premises were opened by the late Lord Mayor and Lady Mayoress (to whom your Committee feel that especial thanks are due) on June 12th last, in presence of a large and distinguished gathering of friends. It had been expected that the building would have been ready three months earlier; but the long frost of last

spring delayed the work, with the consequence
that part of our old premises was let to other
tenants, so that it became necessary to carry on
the Club for some time with greatly straitened
accommodation. This inevitably caused considerable inconvenience and dislocation of the
Club-life, which was increased by the difficulty
and confusion of moving into the new house.

"It is scarcely necessary to state that the new
house is far more commodious and convenient
than the old rooms, affording space for a large
increase of membership, as well as for new
developments of club activity. The allocation
and use of the various rooms must be regarded
as still in the stage of trial and experiment;
and it may possibly be found desirable to
change the present arrangements in some
respects.

"Your Committee think it well to call the
attention of members to the fact that the Club
is the property of the President, who is
personally liable for the debt on the building,
and in whose name the ground lease and all
other contracts are made out. The President
and your Committee are agreed that this
state of affairs can only be considered as
temporary and that the time has come when
a new arrangement should be made. The

nature and terms of such arrangement must be determined between the President and the Committee; but your Committee desire to express their own opinion that the President can on longer be expected to find money for the current expenses of the Club. An institution of this kind cannot be regarded as established upon a sound basis unless it is self-supporting. The President has furnished the rent for more than six years, and has now provided the Club with a new and beautiful house. Your Committee feel that the sum owed to him ought to be repaid as soon as possible, and that the Club should be placed in a permanent, self-supporting and responsible position. To this end your Committee recommend that a Special Committee be now appointed to consider the question and to report to a Special General Meeting called for the purpose.

"*Building Fund.*—It was anticipated in the last report of your Committee that a portion of the cost of the building would have to be raised by mortgage. This has proved to be the case. For this the President, not the members, is responsible. The members were able, however, to collect and contribute a sum of £407 18s. to the Building Fund.

"*Members' Roll.*—The total membership is now 454. The Club-House could comfortably accommodate 600 members; and your Committee are of opinion that no more effective service can at present be rendered to the Club than that of bringing in new members.

"*Wants.*—The chief wants of the Club at present are money and members. So long as the institution is hampered by debt, it is impossible for it to advance and expand, as otherwise would certainly be the case. It is the intention of the President, so soon as the debt is cleared off, to place the building in the care of Trustees, for the purposes of the Club, in the hope of thus securing its permanence, and rendering it independent of his own continuance in his present position. Nothing, however, can be done until the Club is freed from debt, and to bring this about as soon as possible, should be the aim of all who are interested in the place."

One of Shuttleworth's undertakings on behalf of the Club funds, was a lecturing tour in the West. He writes thus in February 1896—

"In Easter week I propose to make a lecturing tour through the principal towns of Cornwall, on behalf of the Building Fund of the Club. I intend telling the story of

'English Hymns and Hymn-tunes,' with illustrations by the principal quintett from our own choir, and the organist as accompanist. The towns at present arranged are as follows : 'Monday, April 6th, Wadebridge ; Tuesday, Bodmin ; Wednesday, Falmouth ; Thursday, Truro ; Friday, Helston ; Monday, Penzance ; Tuesday, St. Austell.' Will all my Cornish friends—I am proud to say I have many— write to their friends in the west, and get them to support this endeavour ?   I have done what I could for Cornwall in my time, and now I am asking my native county to do something for me ; or rather, for an undertaking which is very dear to my heart, and a heavy burden on my shoulders !"

In May 1896 a grant was made to the Club Building Fund, in circumstances which Shuttleworth thus describes : " The Trustees of the London Parochial Charities have voted a grant of £100 to the Club Building Fund.   This is a particularly welcome gift, not only as a generous contribution to our funds, but because it is a handsome recognition, on the part of a public body of the work done by the Club.   I hope other public bodies who have money to dispense, may be induced to follow this good example. The Trustees took over the property of the old City charities, under a scheme of the

Charity Commissioners, and have large powers of administration. This is, I believe, the first instance in which a grant has been given to a social club, as distinct from an educational institution or polytechnic."

An application for a grant from the Corporation funds was subsequently made, in regard to which Shuttleworth said . " I appeared as a petitioner at the bar of the Court of Common Council, some little time back, to beg a grant from the corporation for the Club Building Fund. I was greatly gratified and touched by the singular kindness with which my request was received. Mr. Alderman Treloar, one of our Vice-Presidents, was good enough to present the petition ; Mr. A. A. Wood, a well-known City Nonconformist, seconded its reference to the Finance Committee, in a speech of which I will only say, that it was far too generous ; and other corporators said very kind things. The petition has gone to the Committee, and whether they are able to help the Club or not, I shall never forget the manner in which petition and petitioner were treated by the Corporation. I came out of the Guildhall feeling that I had not lived for twenty years in the City altogether in vain."

A proposal was made by the Members of the
Club that they should meet once a year for
corporate worship; and the first service of
this kind took place on the 26th September,
1897. Writing on this subject, Shuttleworth
said—

"I propose to suggest to the Club Committee, that the 'Club service' in Church,
which was asked for at a General Meeting of
members, shall be held on the afternoon of
Sunday, September 26th, the first Sunday of
the Harvest Festival. My idea is that it should
be a short and simple service, with plain chants
and hymns. I have an idea of trying my hand
at writing a special hymn for the occasion : but
I know from the experience of many failures,
how much harder it is to write a passable hymn
than almost any other kind of verse, and a Club
Hymn presents peculiar difficulties."

At the first Club Service there was an
attendance of some two hundred members, of
whom twenty-five formed the Choir. Shuttleworth addressed the members, taking as his
text the words : "We are members one of
another," and the hymn written for the occasion
was sung to the tune "Kingsley," also composed by Shuttleworth.

HYMN OF THE SHUTTLEWORTH CLUB.

"Fellowship is Heaven."

Father of men, in Whom are one
All humankind beneath Thy sun,
Stablish our work in Thee begun.

Except the House be built of Thee,
In vain the builder's toil must be—
O strengthen our infirmity!

Man lives not for himself alone,
In others' good he finds his own,
Life's worth in fellowship is known.

We, friends and comrades on life's way,
Gather within these walls to pray,
Bless our Club-fellowship to-day!

O Christ, our Elder Brother, Who
By serving man God's Will didst do,
Help us to serve our brethren too.

Guide us to seek the things above,
The base to shun, the pure approve,
To live by Thy free law of love.

In all our work, in all our play,
Be with us, Lord, our Friend, our Stay
Lead onward to the Perfect Day!

Then may we know, earth's lesson o'er,
With comrades missed, or gone before,
Heaven's fellowship for evermore.

The "Club Service" has continued regularly year by year, the addresses being given by the Lord Bishop of London (Dr. Creighton) in 1898, by Mr. G. W. E. Russell in 1899, by Rev. R. R. Dolling in 1900, and by the present Bishop of London in 1901.

Encouraged by his successful application to the Corporation, Shuttleworth in the spring of 1898 endeavoured to interest the City Companies in the work of the Club, but with little result. He says: "After the Corporation helped me so generously in the early part of last year, I sent a petition, identical with that I had addressed to the Court of Common Council, to about twenty-five City Companies. The result was not entirely encouraging. Two kindly responded with ten guineas each, and four with five guineas. One was precluded by its own rules from assisting, since it had made us a liberal grant, when the new Club was being built. Another declined to help a club of any kind, and immediately afterwards (according to the *City Press*), gave £25 to a Boys' Club outside the City. I must try again, I suppose. I dare say I failed to work the thing properly, and trusted too much to the goodness of the cause. But I confess I did think, that a club for City *employés*, which has a successful career of nine years behind it, and now pays its own current expenses, might have appealed to the City Guilds to better purpose than forty guineas. I had hoped to get at least five hundred! Still, the forty guineas went some way towards paying the year's interest on the mortgage; and I am grateful for small mercies, while still hoping for larger ones."

Some of the last words written by Shuttleworth had reference to the Club. Late in September 1899, he said: "The Special General Meeting of the Club, which was called for 21st September, will be remembered as the occasion of an important new departure. It has been felt for some time that the membership of the Club has been changing in character. We are getting older men, and the proportion of members from the City houses has been of late rather smaller than was formerly the case. If this were to become one of the permanent conditions of Club life, one of the main objects of the institution would be nullified.

"The practical difficulty is that with a smaller subscription for all members we could not pay our way. In the hope, therefore, of attracting a considerable number of younger members, more particularly from the City houses, it has now been resolved that members under the age of twenty-three shall pay a subscription of half-a-guinea per annum, and an entrance fee of half-a-crown. I sincerely hope that the new rule may have the desired effect, and bring in a large accession of useful members."

The relations between Shuttleworth and the members of the Club were always most cordial and affectionate. He spared neither time, money, nor labour in the service of those who were of his society. His best work was given freely and fully to the cause of those whose lives, dull and grey from monotony and hard work, he brightened and transformed by his own influence and geniality.

His Literary Lectures attracted large audiences to the Club, and were subsequently given by him in West-End drawing-rooms for the benefit of the Club funds. The principal courses were——

Season	1889–1890	Modern Poets and Poetry.
,,	1890–1891	Shakespeare, his Age and Art.
,,	1891–1892	Poets of the Eighteenth and early Nineteenth Centuries
,,	1892–1893	English Social Reformers.
,,	1893–1894	Studies in Browning.
,,	1894–1895	Further Studies in Browning.
,,	1895–1896	English Novels and Novelists.
,,	1896–1897	The English Drama
,,	1897–1898	Studies in Shakespeare
,,	1898–1899	Some of Shakespeare's Women.

The Club was the last place in which Shuttle-worth appeared before his last illness. As was his usual custom, he was present at the choir-practice on the evening of Friday, 22nd September, 1899, and afterwards visited the Club to greet the members on his return from his holiday visit to Devonshire. On the follow-ing day he was far from well, and never again was he seen in bodily presence in the Club which he had founded and for which he had sacrificed so much. It is the earnest hope of his friends that his plans and aims for the Club may yet be realized, and that this institution may become a permanent feature of the social life of the City, and a lasting memorial to its Founder.

The following note by a young clerk in a Warehouseman's business may well be inserted here—

" Professor Shuttleworth was a success among men in the City — and elsewhere, for that matter—because he understood them.

" He was always so bright and happy, and ever ready to promote the happiness of others, that men, young and old alike, were made to look to him as a friend and brother.

" Men object to clergymen who can't speak or laugh naturally, but they like and respect a

N

priest who can play 'a hundred up' before gathering them round him at Choir-practice or Bible Class.   Certainly in Henry Cary Shuttle-worth, they had a man, unassuming, devoted to healthy recreation, a sound counsellor, and a faithful teacher.

" Every one knows, of course, how much he was bound up in City life, but I don't think it is so generally known, to what extent he worked in and among the various Warehouses and religious classes in them.

" His addresses were always looked forward to and greatly appreciated.   He was very par-ticular as to what went on at these classes when he had to give the address.   A few days before he was due at a well-known Warehouse in St. Paul's Churchyard, he wrote to the young man who had arranged for his coming—' Please arrange not to have extemporaneous prayers —these, and Sankey's hymns, are more than I can stand.'

" He took a deep interest in the hours and conditions of labour in City Warehouses, and, though unable to take any active part himself, yet he obtained powerful aid for the aggrieved, in the dispute between Messrs. Pawsons and Leaf and their clerks in 1899.   It was un-doubtedly due to this aid which he procured, that the men were able to place their case fairly before the public, with the result that their grievances were remedied.

"In this, as in many another instance, he was true to his Christian Socialist principles, and he never hesitated to take the side of the oppressed against Injustice.

"My recollections of Henry Shuttleworth I shall always treasure, because I consider he was a man who lived for the good of others, and by so doing, brought near to our Blessed Lord those who cannot be won by words alone."

The eloquent testimony of Shuttleworth's intimate friend, and former curate, the Rev. F. L. Donaldson, may fitly be added to what has gone before—

"The work for which he made the greatest sacrifices of heart and brain, was work for the young men and women of the City. Ever since he first came, in 1876, to London, he had yearned to do something for them. He felt deeply their need of wholesome fellowship outside their warehouses and offices, and soon after he became rector of this parish he set his hand to the absorbing task of building up both the community and the home in which to lodge it. It should be, he said, a community founded upon the primæval principle : 'Male and female created He them.' He not only deplored the evil of multiplying monster establishments for men, but he lamented the segregation of the sexes. 'What God hath joined together, let not man put asunder.' Such was his principle. And the Club for both men and women, now established in this parish, was the outward development and symbol of this belief. Its confessed success justified the boldness of the attempt; and its witness before the world of the possibility of community life such as this, without scandal or reproach, and with unquestionable advantages of mutual helpfulness and friendship for men and women members, must be invaluable in such an age as ours. The Shuttleworth Club has been and remains a remarkable success, and in large measure has justified that ancient saying written large upon the lintel of its entrance: 'Fellowship is Heaven; the lack of fellowship is Hell.' Sad to say, this success was dearly purchased. To build for business purposes in the City is an undertaking vast indeed; but to build for philanthropy, as a project seemed chimerical. Yet he did it, and did it even upon a large and liberal scale. But some of us knew what incessant labour it entailed upon him. Much of his leisure, and of his substance too, was

absorbed by this institution. The vast responsibility of it weighed constantly upon him
and indirectly shortened his dear life. We
gladly remember that the sacrifice was, once
at least, formally acknowledged. These words
following, taken from a memorial given him by
the society, frankly and beautifully express what
the members knew and felt : '*Your ceaseless
energy and self-denying thoughtful labours, have
firmly founded this centre of helpful recreation
and place of home-like meeting for men and
women of our City of London. We feel most
deeply all we owe to you : and that we may the
plainer prove our gratitude, would leave to your
family some record of your work for us. We
pray that you may be spared long to brighten the
lives around you in the same full measure as
your goodness and learning, fearless vigour and
true manliness have brightened and bettered
ours.*' The debt is here acknowledged and
the sacrifice recorded ; yet the debt was larger
than was suspected even by the inner circle of
his friends. For the work entailed upon him
(heavy incessant work for money) shortened
this splendid life. Lecture succeeded lecture,
sermon succeeded sermon ; article upon article
was written for newspaper and magazine—all
to secure guineas and patronage for the Club.

Surely it were incredible, did we not know it to be true, that a man like this for ten long years should labour late and early, in addition to all his other works, and wear himself out in securing a few paltry hundreds of pounds, in the midst of a city such as this, so vast, so majestic, so rich. Verily it has been said: 'How hardly shall they that have riches enter into the Kingdom of God.'"

Closely connected in its spirit and motive with Shuttleworth's social work for the young men and maidens of the City, was his zeal for the Christian honour of the Stage and of the theatrical profession. Clergymen who, even from the highest motives, meddle with dramatic affairs generally find themselves involved in controversy and not seldom in ridicule. It may therefore be expedient to give Shuttleworth's view of the matter, as reported by one who heard him debate it with an anti-dramatic Nonconformist.

"No class of people known to me have realized the spirit of brotherhood among each other as have the fraternity of the Stage. No broken-down actor, no actress fallen upon evil days, ever appeals in vain to the more fortunate members of their calling. And as to living loosely and intemperately, let me remind you of Ruskin's well-known reply to a similar charge brought against artists in another field. A loose life must tell fatally upon nerves and brain and physique ; so that a man or woman who would excel in the art of the Stage simply cannot afford to be other than rigorously careful and disciplined in mode of living."

He went on to say that there were three great functions which have been and might be discharged by the Drama. The first, that of a religious teacher, which was the original function of the Stage, was now obsolete except in such exceptional cases as the *Passionspiel* of Ober-Ammergau, or the *Parsifal* of Richard Wagner. It might be that in the not far distant future the Stage might again fulfil this, the earliest and highest of its possibilities. But at present it was out of reach.

The second function of the Stage was that of a moral or religious teacher, directly or indirectly. It was perhaps in this respect that the English Stage had advanced most remarkably of recent years. Not long since, one of the first managers in London declared that " Shakespeare spelt ruin." Now the Shakespeare revivals were among the most popular and successful events of the theatrical year.

A new class of play had come to the front, in which an endeavour was made to set forth a moral or a social problem. Such an attempt could only be entered on by discreet and practised hands, and whether or not it was wise to take girls to see them, he had no doubt as to the effect of such plays as these upon men and women. They made thoughtless people think; they preached sermons to ears which the parson could not reach, and the speaker knew of one man at any rate who had more than once thanked God through his tears for the dramatist who conceived, and the actress who interpreted, such a tremendous moral lesson as that of the " Profligate."

But the chief function of the Stage was unquestionably that of amusement, which in its proper place is as true a necessity of life as food or medicine. In every walk of life Dulness is the deadly foe of righteousness, and, in doing battle with this demon, we are dealing heavy blows at the mighty giants of Degradation and Despair.

Coming to the duty of Christians with relation to the Stage, Shuttleworth said that there were three courses open. They might forcibly suppress it. That method had been tried by the Puritans of the seventeenth century, and failed. They might do as Dr. Newman Hall recommended—let it alone, but advise Christian people to keep aloof from it. This meant deliberately handing over a great art, a powerful influence on life, to the less serious and less spiritual section of the community. It also meant impoverishing one's own life, and doing a serious wrong to the dramatic profession and those engaged in it. The only sensible and really religious attitude for Christians to take up was to use the Stage as novels, pictures, and poetry were used, avoiding what might be bad or doubtful, encouraging or helping forward the good. The Church must act upon the world by contact, not by separation ; as " salt," preserving and purifying that with which it mingles ; as "leaven," pervading with its influence and character the whole lump.

Shuttleworth wound up his brilliant address with the charming story of S. Carlo Borromeo, who was engaged in his favourite game of billiards when one of his chaplains proposed the question : " Sir, if the trumpet of the Last Judgment were to sound at this moment, what would you do ? " " Ask the others first, I will answer last," said the Saint. One man said that he would rush away to the chapel and humble himself before God ; another that he would fall on his knees and give himself to prayer ; and so on, till it came to the turn of S. Carlo. " I should go on with my game," he said, " and do my best to make the next stroke a good one. I know it is God's will that I should sometimes take recreation. What could I be doing at that awful moment better than God's will ? "

This high view of the function and value of the drama led Shuttleworth to be an active member of the " Church and Stage Guild." But that he was fully alive to the perils and absurdities which encrusted that well-meant effort, the following letter to a remonstrating friend makes sufficiently clear.

" If we were all committed to Ballet-olatry, the Guild would be at once reduced to the Secretary and half-a-dozen others. He does his level best to try and commit the Guild ; and this year, for the first time, he has a lot of his friends on the Council. But I agree with you rather than with him ; and so far, we have been able to hold our own. Next year I mean to make a great push to get some other people on the Council, yourself among them. I am quite ready to claim for the ballet-ladies the title of artist, and to recognize the beauty of their work—still more, its *possible* beauty. But I am very far from endorsing all that —— has said on the subject."

The striking testimony of Mr. Ben Greet will be read with interest in this connexion—

"Henry Cary Shuttleworth as a playgoer was in his happiest moments; it was not merely a pastime, it was a real recreation with him.

"I first met him about twenty years ago at Amen Court. I felt at once his sympathetic nature with the hand of friendship held out to me of a calling differing in many respects from his own. In all those years I never knew the eyes flash so brightly and the interest more absorbed than when speaking of the Theatre, and the help it could be to the people. We often discussed the possibilities of a 'City' People's Theatre once more, and we even dreamt of the oft-discussed Shakespeare Memorial Theatre being built where the Guildhall School of Music now stands. What a boon it might be to the thousands of young men and women who live near the large ware-houses. He never caught the philanthropist who would take up the idea, but in a way he laid some foundation for such a scheme in the establishment of the Shuttleworth Club, with its

little theatre and social life, and I believe he
would have carried the project of his City
House of Recreation very much farther, for
all healthy pastime was an absolute passion
with the man. I remember well when he was
at St. Paul's on a spare Sunday afternoon, we
started on a jaunt to Richmond by 'bus, no
sooner had we made ourselves comfortable on
the box-seat, and were going off in a fine
sporting style, when who should drive along
in his landau but his Diocesan! A most friendly
greeting from Dr. Temple delighted Henry
Cary Shuttleworth. Some parsons might have
taken refuge behind the driver's broad back,
not so this one. 'I'm delighted the Bishop
saw me. I wish he'd join the National Sunday
League.' He shocked, I believe, some of the
good people of the City as much by his
advocacy of the Drama as a rational and
national recreation as by his other views with
regard to the social life of the people; but we
change even in twenty years. Then the clergy
had to get most of their recreations and their
ritualisms during flying visits to London and
the continent; now almost every town and half
the country-side has its free and open church,
and its theatre or Hall of Recreation, and
every twentieth man one saw at the Lyceum

was a parson, who even occasionally visits the theatre in his own town. It was such men as Henry Cary Shuttleworth who did so much to stamp out the absurd and unnecessary prejudice against the Stage, but there must be some scapegoat for the clergy to beat, or some of their occupation might be gone. But to the point—to go to the play with Henry Cary Shuttleworth was an education in itself. First of all, he worshipped his Shakespeare, as all genuine playgoers do. He knew him as well as Mr. Gladstone knew his Homer, and like the great Statesman—who was, I think, in all things his ideal man—he could give you a line or tell you where it came from at a moment's notice. He loved to discuss the productions and the readings of his favourite actors, such as Henry Irving and Forbes Robertson, or of his favourite actresses, Mrs. Kendal, Mary Anderson, Ellen Terry, Marion Terry, and Amy Roselle Dacre. And then to hear and see him laugh. Why, he would set the whole theatre in a roar. He loved a Pinero comedy with Mrs. John Wood, or a pantomime with Dan Leno, or one of the really funny Gaiety plays with Edward Terry, Fred Leslie, and Nellie Farren; or the Gilbert and Sullivan plays at the Savoy, which he never missed, or

one of the incomparable old English Comedies
of Sheridan and Goldsmith. His visits to
Stratford-upon-Avon were as enjoyable to
him as his visits to Bayreuth, and one of the
regrets of his life was his inability through
illness to see the Passion Play at Ober-
Ammergau. We had talked of this for some
years, but alas! it was not to be. I shall not
forget the delight it was to him to have a long
talk over the Play during those painful days at
Brighton.

"I think he placed almost on a level with
the plays of Shakespeare, the music dramas
of Richard Wagner. Such majesty of language,
wedded to music of so grand and eloquent
a nature, was a never-failing source of real
delight; and whether upon the stage or the
concert platform the enjoyment of it was
supreme, and he hoped the day would come
when we should possess a theatre capable of
producing almost exclusively the masterpieces
in music and drama of all nations of the world,
and a public in our grimy, matter-of-fact
London capable of enjoying them.

"During the latter years of his precious life
visits to the Play had to give place to the
pressure of parish work, and to that zeal for
helping others which some of us, who knew

him best, viewed with a good deal of misgiving.
I fear we are all selfish, and those who work
pretty hard themselves are apt to let others do
the work of fifty people. Such I fear was the
case with this man. Work seemed to him
such a joy, and there was so much he hoped
to do; but in my humble opinion if he had
worked less and given himself a little more
leisure time we might have had him with us
now. Certain it is that during his last years it
was an often-expressed regret that he could
not visit the theatre as often as he wished. In
his time he wrote several admirable essays on
plays which took his fancy, and I remember
one written upon *Claudian*, in which he com-
pared that clever play to a 'parable of Hell,'
making a great stir at the time. He would so
far encourage the cult of the Drama amongst
his people, that he devoted a page of his Parish
Magazine to consideration of some current play.
I believe I am not betraying a confidence in
stating that he either wrote—or collaborated in
—a play on *Esmond*. Thackeray was his
favourite novelist, as Tennyson was his favourite
poet; Dickens and Browning running next, I
fancy. I think I may conclude these few stray
notes by saying that so great was Professor
Shuttleworth's true love of the Drama, that

he often expressed to me a hope that one of his children would become an Actor."

So far we have spoken mainly of Shuttleworth's parochial and social work; but his academical work must by no means be omitted.

In the year 1883 he had been appointed Lecturer in Pastoral Theology at King's College, under the Professorship of Dr. Swete, and when in 1890 Dr. Swete became Regius Professor of Divinity at Cambridge, Shuttleworth obtained the vacant Chair at King's. This was a charge exactly suited to some of his most admirable qualities; and the close contact with young, ardent, and aspiring hearts was a perpetual stimulus and delight to his own perennially youthful nature. Some of the best work of his life was done in the Pastoral Chair at King's College, and some of his closest friendships were those that bound him to his pupils in the art and science of the Christian ministry.

Dr. Wace, formerly Principal of the College, sends this generous tribute to his younger colleague—

"It is a grateful duty to endeavour to pay a slight tribute to my friend, in memory of my happy association with him while I was Principal of King's College. When I entered on that office he was Lecturer in Pastoral Theology, Dr. Swete, now Regius Professor of Divinity at Cambridge, being the Professor in that subject. He became Professor when Dr. Swete went to Cambridge, and I remember with pleasure that I was able to render him some opportune support in the Council when he was elected. His active participation in some of the Liberal political movements of the day had not unnaturally occasioned some doubt whether it would be desirable to give him the increased authority and influence over candidates for Holy Orders which he would exercise in the Chair, but I had learned to know him too well to have any anxiety on that score, and was thankful to be able to give him unreserved confidence. This was not due to any idea of a diminution in his personal sympathy with the movements in question, but to the great loyalty and sense of responsibility which marked his character. He thoroughly appreciated the fact that a position of increased authority in the College entailed increased obligations in the use of his influence, and I knew that his generous sense of honour would effectually restrain him from compromising his Chair or the College with any causes which did not properly concern them. We had a frank ex-

planation on the subject after his appointment ;
and, while it was understood that his personal
action was perfectly unfettered, he voluntarily
undertook to withdraw from those public engagements which might seem inconsistent with
his position in the College. This understanding
he adhered to with the most generous loyalty,
and, though his sympathies on all subjects were
exhibited with the utmost frankness, he maintained a considerate reserve in public action.
This loyalty was one of his most striking
characteristics, and gave a rare value to his
co-operation as a colleague.   He was always
willing to restrain, and even to repress, himself,
eager as his feelings might be, rather than fail
to support his responsible leaders.   In him I
always had one colleague on whom I could
absolutely rely for whole-hearted support in any
decision I had to make, even though his private
opinion might not entirely agree with mine.
Such unreserved generosity is rare in characters
of such energy and earnestness, and I look back
upon his association with me in this respect with
affectionate gratitude.

"But characters of this nature are peculiarly
fitted to elicit the best feelings of young men,
and he aroused in them the same sort of generous
confidence as he exhibited towards others.   His

capacity as a teacher was great, but it was vastly enhanced by his personal influence as a man. His students felt that he was not merely giving them intellectual instruction, but was placing himself side by side with them, as one man with another, and giving them the benefit of his whole experience, both in heart and mind. There was a peculiarity in his manner as a lecturer which helped to convey the impression. It seemed as if he could neither speak nor lecture coolly, like a professor in a chair, sitting above his audience; but almost threw himself at them, body and mind together. His eyes would gleam, and his face betray intense animation, and every gesture showed that the entire nature of the man was at work, and endeavouring to impart his whole conviction to his hearers. His eloquence, which was considerable, was not the eloquence of art, but of natural earnestness, and he seemed to see and feel everything that he said. Yet with all this there was the sense of responsibility to which I have referred, and, however impetuous his expression of his views and feelings, it was never inconsiderate or without due regard to others. He was kind enough to preach sometimes in the weekly services at my church in Cornhill, and the personal reality which was

apparent in every utterance, gave a fresh life
to the moral and religious truths he enforced.
He was everywhere a man speaking to men or
women, and pouring out to them the genuine
beliefs and feelings of a true, pure, simple and
deeply religious nature.   Others will be able to
speak better than I of his influence in his
parish and in society, but I can testify to the
incalculable value of the work he did in King's
College by means of these qualities.   He was
a perennial source of Christian and manly
influence among all classes of students.   Though
his teaching in the college itself was mainly
confined to the theological students, he threw
himself into the social life of all faculties and
departments of the college, and was a welcome
leader in all their meetings and societies.   In
the Ladies' Department at Kensington his
lectures were eagerly attended.   They were
generally on literary and historical subjects,
and the wide human sympathy with which he
treated such topics aroused the enthusiasm of
his hearers.   Though he lectured so much, not
merely in the college, but in private houses, to
raise funds for the work in his parish he had
so deeply at heart, he was always fresh and
vigorous.   In short, no man that I have known
realized so fully or so constantly the Apostolic

HENRY CARY SHUTTLEWORTH   197

ideal : 'Whatsoever things are true, whatsoever things are honest, whatsoever things are
just, whatsoever things are pure, whatsoever
things are lovely, whatsoever things are of good
report, if there be any virtue, and if there be
any praise, think on these things.' He was
always thinking of them, and he made others
think of them, and it is with these things that
his memory will be perpetually associated by
those who knew him."

Enough has now been written to show that,
during his later years, Shuttleworth lived a life
of literally incessant labour.   Even his holidays
were absorbed by preparation for the work
which lay before him when he should return to
London.   He had a numerous family to educate,
and he had made himself financially responsible
for several of the most important institutions
connected with his parish.   He was one of the
most open-handed of men, carrying hospitality
and generosity to the very verge of imprudence.
It was part of his nature that the things on
which he set his heart must be done, and in
order to do them the money must be procured.
On these points he turned a deaf ear to remon-
strance or dissuasion.   So, atop of all the
burdens, social and ecclesiastical, of his parish,—

atop of his professorial duties at King's, and
the reading and thought which they involved,—
he constantly contributed to magazines, newspapers and reviews, and he lectured in all
imaginable places on all imaginable subjects.
For this line of effort he was particularly quali-
fied by his fluency, address, rhetorical skill, and
power of reproducing all he knew in a striking
and attractive form.   There were few more
popular lecturers on literary topics ; and some
extracts from ladies' letters may be cited as
showing the estimation in which he was held.

"His charm as a lecturer seemed to me to
lie in the way in which he threw himself, heart
and soul, into his subject ; and never left it till
he had exhausted it.   He was always so
interested himself that he carried his hearers
with him, and made them feel as he did."

"I have heard Mr. Shuttleworth in several
different courses of lectures, and cannot imagine
a more interesting lecturer, full of pathos and
humour, and he had a very clear and emphatic
delivery.   In his lectures on Browning's *The
Ring and the Book*, I thought him particularly
good ; he brought out so many beautiful ideas
which an ordinary reader of Browning would
have failed to notice, had they not been specially
pointed out.   His lectures certainly enlarged

one's ideas on many subjects. In the pulpit I have never heard any one who has influenced or attracted me in the same way, and his series of sermons on *The Journey of Life* were most impressive and interesting, and left in one a strong feeling of courage and hopefulness. He evidently had a wide knowledge of human nature, and a strong sympathy with human weakness."

"It was my great privilege to be present at many courses of lectures given by our loved and much-esteemed friend, the late Professor Shuttleworth, and I only wish that I could give any adequate expression to the delight they invariably gave us. It mattered not what the subject might be, whether from Browning or Shakespeare or the less inspiring theme of Church History, etc., the same charm prevailed. Each character lived before one, touched by the marvellous insight of his comprehensive mind and intense sympathy with whatever he took in hand. His memory too was a marvel to all who heard his unfailing flow of language. To me the predominant note of his great life's teaching was his unique combination of intense human sympathies with the finest intellectual gifts, which irresistibly drew to his lectures a most varied circle of hearers, to many of whom his words were an inspiration, as leading them to a more earnest, a truer, higher estimate of life and its responsibilities, and also to its fuller enjoyment. To have listened to him as to a teacher and to have known him as a friend is one of the most precious possessions of my later life."

That Shuttleworth's was a life of sustained, manifold, and to a great extent exterior, activity, has been sufficiently shown by what has gone before ; but that it had a deeper side could never be doubted by those who knew him intimately. A layman, who was closely associated with him both at St. Paul's and at St. Nicholas, writes—

"His solemn earnestness in things spiritual is an impression which will ever remain in the hearts of those to whom he ministered. No time can eradicate it, and yet no words can express it. One thinks of it now standing at the foot of

'the great world's altar-stairs,
That slope through darkness up to God.'

One sees that well-remembered form in priestly garments in the Light beyond, and, like a far-off echo, comes to me, 'Lift up your hearts !' *Lift up your hearts.* It mattered not whether those words were sung or echoed among the lofty arches of St. Paul's, or at the altar of his own church. It was God's command to lift up our hearts above the care and turmoil of this life, and it was Henry Cary Shuttleworth's message to us all, in faith, fear or love, and the watchword of his own life"

A young clergyman to whom Shuttleworth showed serviceable kindness at a critical juncture, sends this interesting memorandum—

" He was often accused, by those who were not in sympathy with his methods, of putting social experiments in the place of Christianity, and attracting people to church by music and literary lectures instead of by preaching the Gospel; and to those who knew the church merely as outsiders or casual visitors such a criticism might easily appear in some measure justified, especially in the later years of his life. But no solid work can be done on such a basis, since people soon weary of mere attractions. It is true, I think, that as time went on the motive force that lay behind all that was permanent at St. Nicholas was less explicitly set forth in words; but from the beginning to the end that force was the power that springs from the belief in the Incarnation. It was this that really drew people to the church and kept them there, little as they may in many cases have realized the fact themselves. It was on this belief that the work of the Rector's earlier years at St. Barnabas, Oxford, was openly based, and I could trace much of the strength of the work at St. Nicholas to the tradition of that church, in which others besides Professor Shuttleworth have found their first expression of that belief. The value of a City church is not measured by 'success,' however much crowded congregations may strike the popular imagination. The City is to the world of commerce much what Oxford is to the intellectual life of England. Its population is largely a fleeting one; numbers of young men come up from the country to live together in it for a few years and then, as travellers in the provinces or as residents in the suburbs, carry the ideals they have formed at the centre of the business world throughout the ranks of the middle classes of the whole of England. So it is that the condition of real success in a City church is apparent failure. It is among those who attend it for a time and then leave it to carry the lessons they have learned within its walls out into the world, handing them on to others in that commerce of ideas which consciously or unconsciously must accompany the life of trade, that the real work is done, and no one can tell the value of all that the Rector did in all those years of his life at St. Nicholas in ways that left nothing to show, but are secretly remembered by hundreds in all parts of the world."

Here is another testimony to the same effect.

"Shuttleworth was a man to whom every one felt that they could go with the greatest confidence when, in some serious crisis of life, the need was felt of sound and kindly advice. The amount of good that he did in this way is known but to the few of his more intimate friends, to whom he would on rare occasions, and without breaking any confidence, or mentioning names, speak of these cases. If any one had fallen into a scrape, or got into a difficult position, or done something that threatened disaster, or wanted advice as to some new step in life they were contemplating, all such went to him, on the quiet; and I can well understand why. He knew life so well, so fully appreciated its difficulties and temptations, that any one could feel secure in talking to him about the most private matters; sure of never being misunderstood, or condemned from the artificial standpoint of complacent self-righteousness. He would never condone anything really wrong; anything mean, selfish, or false to truth or love; but, though he might condemn the act, he would never crush the man, or cast him off from friendship and send him away despairing. Many whom he had thus saved, by his brotherly sympathy and manly advice, from the downward path, told me of it afterwards. Some cases he told me of himself, but the most, I expect, will never be known in this world."

The Rev. C. N. Kelly, who succeeded Shuttleworth in the Rectory of St. Nicholas, sends this generous tribute—

"Since I have been at the church I have learnt the true value of Shuttleworth's work. Apart from the club, guilds, and services which I found in such excellent working order, flagging only from his very long illness and loss of his personal and almost magic influence, I have had almost daily proof of the reality and abiding results of his work in the characters and lives of those who came under his power. Rich, poor, highly-educated and very simple-minded people, all seem to have been greatly influenced by him for lasting good. Now a very poor woman writes to me asking me to accept sixpence towards his memorial, adding the words, 'God rest his soul, he did so much for me!' Now a highly-educated person whom I casually meet says, 'Have you succeeded Professor Shuttleworth? I never

came to London without going to his church,
and I never heard him preach without learning
and remembering much. He always seemed
to know my spiritual difficulties and to meet
them, and he fortified his views by his wonderful memory and happy power of quotation from
other useful and poetic thinkers in a way I
never knew any one else do so aptly.'

"What work is now carried on at St.
Nicholas has nearly all had its start and impetus
from Shuttleworth, and I always feel of those
who work there now, 'other men have worked,
and ye have entered into their labours.'"

The exuberant and varied energy which
marked Shuttleworth's life from beginning to
end could only have been possible to a very
strong constitution. Indeed, perfect health
was one of the most conspicuous characteristics
of the man. It displayed itself in his elastic
vigour, in his bounding step, in his ruddy face
and gleaming eye and raven-black hair. He
looked always ten years younger than his age;
and any one, taking stock of his appearance,
would certainly have said: "That man has
never had a day's illness in his life." There
was indeed some tradition that in school-days
a weakness of the spine had prevented him

from excelling in those athletic exercises which
he loved; but all traces of such weakness, if
it ever existed, had disappeared before he went
up to Oxford. In middle life he began to show
some signs of a gouty tendency, but these
slight attacks seemed to be the safety-valves
of a too-intense vitality. Tempted by the consciousness of unusual strength, he did the work
of at least two ordinary men, and most of it
was done against time and at the highest pressure. Towards the year 1898 those who were
nearest to him fancied that they began to see
signs of wear and tear. He was overstrung
and overwrought. Social engagements multi-
plied upon him, and, in his eagerness to secure
fresh friends for his parish and its institutions,
he sacrified those restful evenings in his own
study or drawing-room which so often stand
between a hard-worked man and physical
breakdown. To take work easily, to let things
slide, to saunter or loll, or slacken speed or
knock off engagements, were obvious and often-
suggested remedies; but unfortunately they
were to Shuttleworth moral impossibilities.
He was in a thoroughly fatigued and exhausted
condition when, on the 1st August, 1899, he
left home for his holiday. That holiday was
spent partly in Switzerland, partly in Devon-

shire, and partly at his brother's Rectory in
Cornwall. Here he preached at the Harvest
Festival, and that Sermon was his last act of
public ministry. On the 20th September he
returned to London ; presided over a Meeting at the Shuttleworth Club next evening, and
on the following day conducted the usual Choir-
Practice. When Sunday came he was ill in
bed with a headache and a high temperature.
The first and most natural notion of his friends
was that he had been attacked by influenza.
Days went by with neither aggravation nor
abatement of his symptoms, and then the
ominous word " typhoid " began to be whispered.
But weeks went on, and, although the fever
continued, no specifically typhoidal symptoms
declared themselves. He did a good deal of
his work and correspondence from his sick-bed ;
and, on Christmas Day, he was able to receive
the Holy Communion from the hands of his colleague, the Rev. Clement Rogers, who brought
the Blessed Sacrament from the church, while
the congregation continued in silent intercession
for their stricken Rector.

About this time the doctors fell back upon
the convenient theory of blood - poisoning,
probably picked up in Cornwall, perhaps due
to some defect in the drainage of St. Nicholas

Rectory. In order to place the patient in the
healthiest possible surroundings, it was determined in January 1900 to remove him to
Brighton. The journey was safely accomplished, and at Brighton he remained until
September. He was now helpless from the
waist down; but early in the spring a new
and most unfavourable symptom declared itself.
Abscesses formed in the region of the spine,
and before long it became evident that there
was a curvature of the spine just between the
shoulders. From that time onwards he could
not stand, nor even so much as raise himself
in his bed. He suffered no pain, although a
great deal of discomfort; his spirits were still
buoyant, and his patience was remarkable. He
energetically declined to be treated as though he
were dangerously ill. When a friend proposed
a visit, he said, "Not if it is to be a farewell."
He talked hopefully of returning to work in
London, and said that, though he felt he should
never be able to stand again, he should be able
to preach sitting. He spoke often and cheer-
fully of his family and their prospects, and,
when talking to a friend about his eldest boy,
he said, with characteristic peremptoriness,
"Whatever happens, he must go to Oxford."
Indeed, it was a marked characteristic of his

illness that, instead of being dispirited and depressed, he seemed to see both the present and the future through a rose-coloured mist of cheerful fancies.

As the long-continued stay at Brighton had done no tangible good, Shuttleworth determined to return to London. Meanwhile the Rectory was in the hands of workmen, and, yielding to the advice of doctors, though sadly against his own inclination, he became an in-patient at King's College Hospital on the 27th September. In the hospital he was surrounded by all that skill and kindness and devotion could do. Physicians, nurses and friends vied with one another in good offices. But, in spite of all, he visibly and rapidly lost strength. Before long it became apparent to others—but whether to himself or not we shall never know—that the end was approaching.

On the 22nd October, 1900, he talked to the editor of this memoir about the General Election then in progress, and when his friend pleaded, as an excuse for not standing, that he was growing old and lazy, the dying man replied, with characteristic energy, " No, no, I can't allow you to call yourself old or lazy yet." This conversation was perhaps his last contact with the outer world. Unconsciousness soon set in, and on the 24th October he quietly fell asleep in the Lord.

Thus died Henry Cary Shuttleworth, having lived on "this dim spot which men call Earth" exactly fifty years. I am persuaded that those who knew his work, whether at Oxford or in London, will feel that they hear his very voice speaking to them in the words with which he concluded the Three Hours' Service at St. Barnabas, on Good Friday, 1875—

"When the hour comes for us to close the last chapter of our life; the winding-up of all things, the rush of unknown darkness on our spirits, the awful wrench from all we have loved on earth—oh, brethren, I ask you and I ask myself, fearfully and humbly, *what* will then be finished? When it is finished, what will it be? A life of self-gratification and sin? A life of mere money-seeking? An unfinished, incomplete, imperfect life? Or will it be,—*Father, I have finished the work which Thou gavest me to do?*"

They are words worthy of a workman who never spared himself in the task to which he had set his hand. Farewell, true friend of all these years, bright comrade, gallant soldier. May we meet once more, and meet for ever, in the Eternal Blessedness.

EPILOGUE

" But above all, beyond the things he did, thank God for the man, for him himself, for what he was as well as for what he did. For only by being what he was could he have done the things he did. Remember his amazing industry which never flagged ; for even when he rested, it was but to plan and scheme his future works Remember his loyalty to friends, to whom he clave in weal and woe with a faithfulness unsurpassed in my experience. Remember his generosity, prodigal to a fault, yet spontaneous, and so kindly that it must have meant a great and noble heart, and was besides a glorious witness in a world in which 'to get' and not 'to give' is deemed the only safe ideal. Remember his magnificent enthusiasm, his burning zeal for God and Good. Of him in view of his ceaseless labours it might well be said : 'The zeal of Thine house hath eaten me up.' Remember his idealism, and how he followed with prophetic sight the visions God vouchsafed him, interpreting them to us that we might know them too. Remember the pureness and simplicity of his life. Touching the world at so many points, he yet remained without a single serious taint ; a friend of publicans and sinners, yet amongst them without reproach ; loving many with affection warm and strong, yet always pure and good ;

anxious for the joy of others, yet in his own recreations, and even in his daily meat and drink, so restrained and temperate. Remember his theology, so stately and yet so comprehensive, after the manner of the Caroline divines he loved · so cultured and yet so warm, like that of his modern masters, Maurice and Charles Kingsley. And as you gather up all these threads into the golden cord which binds the soul of Henry Shuttleworth to the feet of God, render thanks to Him and praise Him for such a life as this!

"And being thankful, also pray. Blend with your prayer for him a plea for those who mourn and miss him most, his nearest, his dearest and his best. For his children, that they may reproduce the virtues and graces of their father; for his wife, who loved him most of all, that she may find God's most holy grace of consolation in her cup of sorrow, and see God's rainbow in the clouds. And for him, that his soul, resting in light and peace, may be cleansed of whatever faults remained, by the merits of our Saviour. Pray, pray for his soul, for his repose and perfecting in Christ, for his peace and illumination, for his progress from strength to strength, and for his final glory and joy in Heaven. *Requiescat in pace per Christum Dominum nostrum. Amen.*" [1]

[1] From a Memorial Sermon, by the Rev. F. L. Donaldson

APPENDIX

THE following Appreciation of Shuttleworth, from the pen of Mr. Sydney S. Pawling, originally appeared in *The Outlook*. It seems to state so clearly and concisely his true character and aim in life, that all sympathetic readers of this Memoir will be glad to have it preserved

In the inner circle of friends of the late Henry Cary Shuttleworth, two distinct, even paradoxical, impressions become of necessity paramount. The first, induced by sorrow at his too early death, is an impression of tragedy ; the tragedy of a life sacrificed by overwork to establish and carry out ideals. The second is an impression, or instinct, not of tragedy, but of triumph, created by the remembrance of his outspoken and inspiring conviction of fuller and more perfect opportunities for work after death. His ideals were high, and consequently in striving to carry them out his work was hard —an idealist all through, but ever a worker to fulfil his imaginings. And time has incontestably proved them good. Humanity was his field, and to its well-being he brought a boundless enthusiasm, a cultured mind, and indomitable effort. All the obituary notices in their bald statements of fact miss, as they were bound to miss, that measure of appreciation felt by those whose privilege it was to have closer knowledge of the attempt and effective realization, in his work of unselfish service to others.

Appointed in 1883 when in his thirty-fourth year to Wren's beautiful church of St. Nicholas Cole Abbey, he found that atmosphere of disuse and neglect which was becoming synonymous with City churches and City parishes. The old-time needs of such parishes existed no longer; changes in the customs of life and living had led many to clamour for their discontinuance or sequestration. Examples of large endowments to certain churches with an average congregation of three people had become a familiar grievance with reformers of superficial knowledge; and to many, more seriously equipped, it seemed that some radical change was imperative. Shuttleworth quickly recognized that the needs and opportunities had not ceased with the perforced dwindling of residents or congregation; the requirements were different, but not destroyed. He realized rather that the greater stress of business life in its ever-increasing rush and difficulty gave him the fuller opportunity and could make his church the centre of an added dignity of purpose. He saw that at no time in its history did the City of London stand so much in need of churches in its midst; that never before had its citizens and its workers so largely needed the help and inspiration such churches should offer. His task was not the normal carrying on of an existing tradition, for he was the pioneer of a new movement; he had to attack it alone, and create new methods. But neither his great capacity for work nor his exceptional attainments as a musician and scholar could have succeeded alone. It was his individuality as a man which made the accomplishment of his work possible. He drew people to him by the cardinal qualities of courage and gentleness; he was teacher and friend in one; a comrade as well as a priest; a master in theology, but not a theologian as the word is commonly used. He loved life, and gave all that was best of himself to help others to love it too. It was inevitable that he should have critics, but he could hardly have had any enemies. His church quickly became a centre of beautiful service.   He trained and conducted a voluntary choir of men and women, and whatever criticism the innovation may have occasioned, it was silenced when judged by its result.   There may have been more ornate services in London, but there were none with a greater distinction of reverence and beauty.   His tact and personality quickly drew men and women helpers from City firms and elsewhere ; some lived in the City itself, many came from remoter districts.   And he was loyally served.   Worshippers at the church enrolled themselves as members.   St. Nicholas and its services were the foundation of all developments arising from its Rector's large and varied ideas and resources. In all the extended schemes of clubs, societies, guilds, lectures, and so forth, it was Shuttleworth's chief anxiety that the church should be and remain the bed-rock of all effort.   He persistently recalled the necessity of the utmost recognition of the spiritual origin of every ambition and attainment.   It was not difficult to realize that, in helping forward the social happiness of others by providing opportunities for companionship and friendship, the danger of a solely secular appeal had to be guarded against.   The Rectory from his earliest occupancy was a haven of hospitality, an open home of taste and refinement amid gaunt warehouses and the pressing toil of endless workers. It is not too much to say that all were welcome, and all could share, not only in the pleasures of art, music, and stimulating talk, but in the assured sympathy and comradeship of a man whose passion was humanity. Success came, and success made a wider scope essential. Time, and a more detailed experience of the requirements and opportunities, induced the Rector, with almost quixotic courage, to take upon himself the burden of founding a club near the church. The success of the Shuttleworth Club at the present moment is in cheerful contrast to the gloomy expectations of many who felt the task too onerous and too full of difficulty for one man to undertake. Such expectations cannot be censured, for the obstacles might well appear insurmountable. But the Club was established, decorated, and furnished; and its prompt and enthusiastic appreciation, by those for whom its founder initiated and planned it, was apparent from its opening. It is only too obvious that the financial responsibility which the Rector undertook in his customary whole-hearted manner was a great and grave one. The capital he gave to it is the most precious capital of all, and demands the greatest sacrifice, for he freely gave the unceasing energy of his heart and brain. Undaunted by the absence of any really adequate support from the rich men of the richest city in the world, who trade within a small radius of the church, he earned by continual series of Lectures on Art and Literature, a sum of money large in its total, and large enough to meet the great expenses of establishment. The strain and tax on his vitality must have been enormous. Already a man with few opportunities for leisure, this superimposed responsibility gradually absorbed his strength.

Of the lectures themselves, it can be said that had he been by profession, as he was by accomplishment, "a man of letters," they would have taken a distinguished place in criticism. To particularize, it may be that the courses on Browning stand out as his best work—they were marked by a simple directness of appreciation and a characteristic grappling with the dramatic issues, which in the best sense educated his hearers.

Although the building up and the practical and material outfit of the Club House was only possible through the financial result of this extra work, the claims on the founder of it had

only begun.   Probably he had hardly foreseen
that, for the Club to fulfil his desire, he must
still further give the vitalizing influence of his
own presence and character.   In truth, he gave
with a full hand.   It was not that he dominated
the many interests which sprang up, but from
him radiated the force or inspiration to achieve
them.   An ardent cricketer and excellent judge
of the game, his presence in the Club team was
the mainspring of the prominent position it
soon gained in club cricket.   The same held
good in the debates, the whist and chess
tournaments, the lectures, the concerts, the
library, and all the manifold interests for helping the members, who were ever his friends, to
a larger happiness in their lives.   The ceaseless
pressure of the fight told at last even on a
strong constitution and a temperament of
exceptional activity.   The annual holidays
were looked forward to with a longing which
must have been little short of anxiety, and were
enjoyed with the zest which hard work provides.
It cannot be said that they were times of entire
rest, for the tired worker was keenly desirous
of being in touch with contemporary movement
in the intellectual, social, and political life of
the day.   Hard reading and study to a large
extent took the place of a more expedient

idleness; the claims of learning were to him imperative, in view of the demands upon him as a teacher.

The inevitable breakdown came twelve months ago, after sixteen years of work as Rector of St. Nicholas. He died on October 24, 1900. By a strange coincidence, his burial from the City he had loved so well took place within a few hours of the time arranged for the triumphal return of the citizen soldiers from South Africa. Some of those to whom his own life-work was devoted had lost their lives in the service of their country, and it is not straining the facts to say that Shuttleworth, too, had no less actually spent and given his life in carrying forward the flag of a true and living citizenship.

One thing remains, which can only be indicated with a reverent and respectful sympathy, and yet which cannot be ignored: in the many-sided work to which he ungrudgingly gave himself, it was always known to his friends that the innermost ideal was in his home. And only by that innermost ideal can those who knew and loved the man measure the loss.

He lived and died a staunch Churchman —an ecclesiastic without bigotry—a broad-minded, warm-hearted gentleman. He needs no memorial, for he has fashioned his own, in the hearts and enduring remembrance of the men and women to whom he gave so much.

INDEX

Richard Clay & Sons, Limited, London & Bungay

CPSIA information can be obtained at www.ICGtesting.com
Printed in the USA
BVOW09s0957130515

400213BV00016B/197/P

9 781176 660106